Celebrate! with Little Quilts

That Patchwork Place®

Alice Berg ★ Mary Ellen Von Holt ★ Sylvia Johnson

Credits

Editor-in-Chief .... Barbara Weiland
Technical Editor .... Sally Schneider
Managing Editor .... Greg Sharp
Copy Editor .... Tina Cook
Proofreader .... Leslie Phillips
Design Director .... Judy Petry
Text and Cover Designer .... Amy Shayne
Production Assistant .... Claudia L'Heureux
Technical Illustrator .... Carolyn Kraft
Illustration Assistant .... Lisa McKenney
Decorative Art .... Barb Tourtillotte
Photographer .... Brent Kane
Photography Assistant .... Richard Lipshay

Celebrate! with Little Quilts
© 1995 by Alice Berg, Mary Ellen Von Holt,
and Sylvia Johnson
That Patchwork Place, Inc., PO Box 118
Bothell, WA 98041-0118 USA

Printed in Hong Kong
00 99 98 97 96 95   6 5 4 3 2

Library of Congress Cataloging-in-Publication Data
Berg, Alice,
    Celebrate! with little quilts / Alice Berg, Mary Ellen Von
Holt, Sylvia Johnson.
        p.   cm.
    ISBN 1-56477-108-3
    1. Quilting—Patterns. 2. Patchwork—Patterns. 3. Doll
quilts. 4. Crib quilts.
I. Von Holt, Mary Ellen.   II. Johnson, Sylvia. III. Title.
TT835.B3557 1995
746.46'0228—dc20   95-35157
                                        CIP

Dedication

Little Quilts recently celebrated its tenth year in business. We are grateful to our families, and to the friends and fellow quilters who made our journey so memorable and happy. Never did we dream that we would have so many opportunities or that we would meet such wonderful people along the way. This book is dedicated to all of you with our thanks, love, and friendship.

Acknowledgments

We couldn't have done it without:
Our Little Quilt staff: Karin Snyder, Pam Marshall, Millie Ore, and Jeannine Hartman.
Our rug hooking teachers and experts: Mary Floyd, Sandy Gilliam, and Mary Paul Wright.
Our rug hooker, Lita McCormick of Art For Your Soles, Atlanta, Georgia.
Our computer consultant, Susan Upchurch.
North American Bear Co., Inc., Chicago, Illinois.
Our quilter, Janet Rawls. She lives in Conyers, Georgia, and is the wife of a cartoonist and the working mother of two college students. Her skill and friendship are greatly appreciated.
The wonderful homes of:
Wally and Alice Berg,
Ron and Mary Ellen Von Holt,
Butch and Sylvia Johnson,
Charlie and Karin Snyder, and
Harold and Rosemary Youmans.

That Patchwork Place®

MISSION STATEMENT

WE ARE DEDICATED TO PROVIDING QUALITY PRODUCTS THAT ENCOURAGE CREATIVITY AND PROMOTE SELF-ESTEEM IN OUR CUSTOMERS AND OUR EMPLOYEES.

WE STRIVE TO MAKE A DIFFERENCE IN THE LIVES WE TOUCH.

That Patchwork Place is an employee-owned, financially secure company.

Contents

Introduction

As we write this book, Little Quilts is celebrating its tenth anniversary. Throughout the years we have made every effort to make special days memorable, and we try not to let business get in the way. Our children have grown up, friends have moved away, and several "big" birthdays have come and gone. Time seems to pass quickly. Celebrations become our best memories, and we try to give them our personal touch.

We have so many opportunities to celebrate that sometimes it is overwhelming. Births, graduations, marriages, anniversaries, special achievements, and holidays are just the beginning of the list. As quilters we can always provide a perfect tribute for these times. With pieces of cloth and a needle and thread, we make memories into quilts.

We have made quilts for our children to celebrate their graduations, choosing special events or their college colors as the theme. We have also made quilts to mark anniversaries for ourselves and our parents, choosing themes like "our song" or a favorite room. We have often said, "Give us a theme and we'll wear it out completely!"

One occasion we have been happy to celebrate is the choice of Atlanta as the location of the 1996 Summer Olympics. To mark the occasion, quilters from around the state of Georgia are making quilts that will be given to selected officials from each participating country. Four hundred quilts will be presented. Among those will be one from each of us.

In our book *Little Quilts, All Through The House* we introduced ourselves and our ideas for making "Little Quilts" and decorating with them. Continue with us as we celebrate our love for quiltmaking.

Alice Berg
Mary Ellen Von Holt
Sylvia Johnson

Alice Berg

All my life I have been an "idea" person. Whatever the occasion, I could always think of something to do. As a child, I built playhouses, organized games, and sold lemonade. Later, in school, there was hardly an event in which I was not involved. Thinking of themes and decorating appropriately is my calling.

My childhood birthday parties were simple family gatherings, but when I was nine, my friend had a party that I have never forgotten. It was an afternoon dress-up affair. The table was beautifully set, with fresh flowers, cloth napkins, and china plates, just as it would have been for grown-ups. Eight little girls, all on their best behavior, sat around that table. I felt like a princess; my friend must have felt like a queen.

Everyone needs to feel special. Now, as a quilter, I am able to give family and friends lasting memories made of cloth.

Mary Ellen Von Holt

While growing up in the Midwest, celebrations of all types were common in my family. Although I had only three brothers, I had more than twenty-five first cousins, lots of aunts and uncles, and special grandparents. My family's social life revolved around relatives' birthdays, graduations, weddings, and other celebrations.

I have always enjoyed making handcrafted gifts, which seem more personal than purchased ones. Little Quilts are the perfect gift for family and friends. Over the past ten years I have made many of them to commemorate special events.

Celebrate with Us

Lately I have been making gifts of a different fiber—wool. For the past two years I have been "hooked" on primitive rug hooking, and I now enjoy making little rugs as gifts for friends and even for myself. Because these rugs have caught our imagination and because they perfectly complement Little Quilts, we have included directions for three Little Rugs in this book.

Sylvia Johnson

The excitement of holidays, celebrations, special moments, and seasonal changes always makes me think of friends, family, and home. These are times to decorate, or to remember someone with a gift. For me, these activities began in elementary school.

Every February I took a shoe box to school. I covered it with red and pink construction paper, doilies, hearts, and stickers. On February 14, my valentine mailbox was ready for cards and my "penny" valentines were ready for delivery. We had heart-shaped cookies, nut baskets, and punch for refreshments. I treasured my valentines for a long time. It was a simple celebration, but it was important to me.

Today, I have traded the construction paper, paste, and doilies for fabric, thread, and buttons. My valentines have become quilts, which my family and friends can enjoy and pass on with warm feelings.

What Is a Little Quilt?

Not to be confused with miniature quilts, a Little Quilt is a small version of a full-size quilt. It is made just like a large quilt, with blocks, borders, binding, and quilting. The pieces are easy to handle, you need only basic supplies, and you can use a variety of construction methods. We have included our favorite quiltmaking techniques in "General Directions" on pages 20–25.

SECRETS FOR MAKING LITTLE QUILTS

★ Make a Little Quilt as you would a full-size quilt, just smaller in scale.
★ Use fabrics you have on hand, slightly uncoordinated and scrappy.
★ Use thin batting.
★ Use simple quilting and tea dyeing to produce an aged look.
★ Press the quilts when they are finished, and display them proudly.

USING YOUR LITTLE QUILTS

The softness of quilts is welcome in any decor. Making the quilts featured in this book is easy, and using them throughout your home makes them fun to have. Look at the photographs of our rooms on pages 13–19 to find new ways to display your Little Quilts. You can hang a quilt on the wall like a textile painting, place it on a table or chair, hang it on a peg, or drape it in a basket. The same quilt can be used in many different ways. Move quilts around to create new arrangements, grouping them with other objects by color, or seasonal or holiday themes.

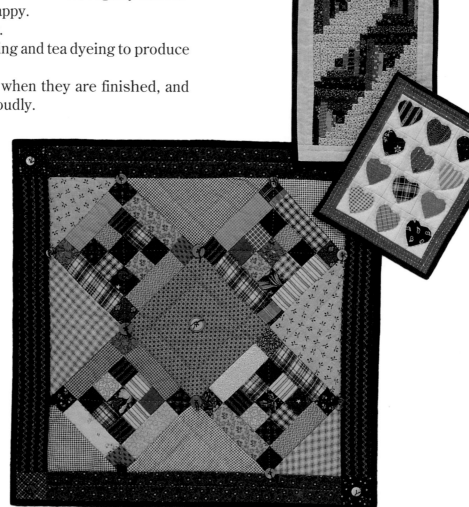

There is a difference between small and miniature.

Our first Little Quilts were a result of our search for authentic doll quilts like the ones we saw in magazines. We soon found that these quilts are not as readily available as we had thought. Reproducing the doll quilts we saw and designing our own eventually led us into a full-time business.

We love making new Little Quilts, but we still want to own the old ones. As we travel and hunt at antique fairs, we always keep on the lookout for these treasures.

COLLECTING ANTIQUE DOLL QUILTS

Keep these pointers in mind if you plan to collect antique doll quilts.
- ★ Buy from a reputable dealer.
- ★ Check the binding. If it appears too new it might indicate that the piece was cut from an old quilt, and there are fifty more just like it.
- ★ Look at the backing fabric and the quilting. It should be in keeping with the rest of the quilt and not look too new.
- ★ Ask dealers for the history of a piece. Look for dates or initials on the quilt.
- ★ Check the scale of the block. It should be small and in keeping with a doll-size bed.

You may find a doll quilt that doesn't meet "museum" standards but is appealing to you. By all means, buy it. Doll quilts are not perfect pieces. They were made for little girls to play with or by little girls as work pieces to learn needlework skills. If the quilt tugs at your heart, overlook the rules and enjoy it.

There are directions for reproducing two antique doll quilts. For a successful reproduction, choose your fabrics carefully, use very thin quilt batting, and give the quilt a gentle "tea bath" to make it look old. See "Tea Dyeing" on page 25.

MAKING DOLL QUILTS

Many doll quilts were originally made from leftover quilt blocks. You can successfully make a Little Quilt by sewing together blocks you have collected. Cut the blocks to size if necessary, and don't worry if the seams don't match. Keep the quilting simple.

Look for old blocks while antique shopping, especially simple Four Patch or Ninepatch blocks. Avoid using large blocks in doll quilts.

You can make wonderful Little Quilts with extra blocks saved from projects in this book. Work on your design wall and create an original! Use strips from your stash for borders and to fill in spaces. (See "More Strips!" on page 12.)

Keep extra half-square triangle blocks, Ninepatches, and other small blocks in a basket. You will be surprised at what you can do with your leftover bits and pieces.

CRIB QUILTS

One folk-art piece that collectors treasure is the crib quilt. These small bedcoverings for children date back centuries.

Crib quilts were made to celebrate a birth or to mourn the loss of a child. Grandmothers often made them, as they had more time to devote to the elaborate workmanship that is often evident in these small pieces.

Surviving crib quilts are prized possessions of museums and collectors. They are often displayed on the walls of homes, offices, and galleries, and their value continually increases. Our interest in children's quilts has led us to study early crib quilts. We have included several crib quilt projects in this book. Use our ideas and combine them with yours to make a special quilt for your collection.

A quiet place to rest and reflect.

In *Little Quilts* we divulged our secret for giving quilts an aged look while using today's fabrics. The key is the use of "magic" fabrics. As we studied old quilts, certain fabrics caught our attention. Many of these were simply common to the time they were made; others stood out because they had faded to a new color. Burgundy red often became pale purple and brown faded to soft tan. Certain colors, such as bubble gum pink, seemed to stay alive and add sparkle to the scrap quilt. We call these our "magic" fabrics.

Some of the fabrics we list in the "magic" category may be colors you are uncomfortable using. When you shop for fabric, it is certainly more fun to purchase pleasing colors and cheerful fabrics. But if you add "magic" fabrics to your scrap quilts in small quantities, you will make them much more interesting. Surprise yourself with new color choices. The fabrics shown here are examples of "magic" fabrics. Fabric availability changes constantly, so feel free to substitute any similar print or plaid, keeping in mind the "magic" fabric colors.

Black—prints, plaids, and fabrics with black in them

Plaids and Stripes—all types

Bubble Gum Pink—a "thirties" pink known by various names

Purple—in prints and small geometric designs

Brown—shades such as cinnamon and dark brown

Mustard Gold—several different prints

Tan—"nothing" prints (tan designs on light backgrounds)

"Magic" fabrics, inspired by the colors found in antique quilts.

Fabric and Supplies

Small amounts of many different fabrics are important ingredients for making Little Quilts. These "scrappy" quilts are appealing because they resemble doll quilts made from fabric leftovers. A doll quilt was often a little girl's first attempt at quiltmaking, and she worked with what was on hand.

Keep these pointers in mind when choosing fabric:

★ Choose 100% cotton fabrics from your collection, prewashed and pressed.

★ Some fabrics are not suitable for Little Quilts. Large-scale contemporary prints are difficult to include, but we know that just as we say this, someone will turn out a fabulous Little Quilt contrary to this rule.

★ Choose from tiny prints, plaids, stripes, and small geometric designs. Muted tones work best. Avoid large-scale designs or fabrics that look too "now."

★ Use reproduction prints to get a "feedsack," "thirties," or other period look.

★ Emphasize a patriotic theme with red, white, and blue fabrics.

★ Once you have selected the basic colors, add fabrics from each color group that are lighter and darker in intensity. Instead of plain muslin, use the tan fabrics we call "nothing prints," shown on page 9.

★ Mix in some "magic" fabrics. These colors add interest and give the quilt an aged look.

★ Use occasional "electric" fabrics in small amounts. These bright colors add sparkle. Use these fabrics more than once in a quilt so that they don't stand out.

1. Start with a theme—red, white, and blue. 2. Add values and more prints—red, blue, and tan. 3. Add "magic" colors. Now we're ready!

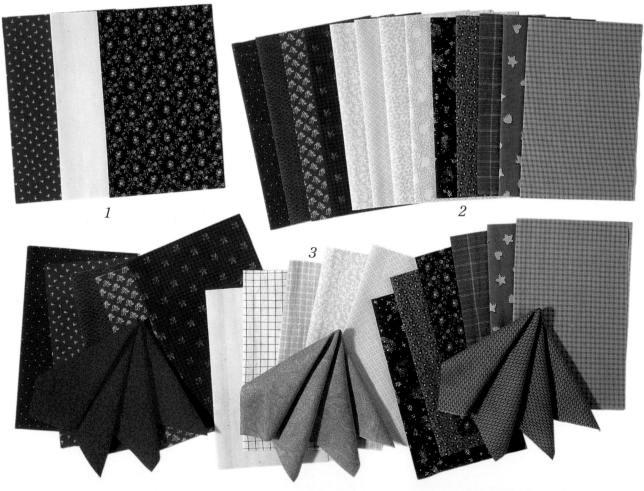

1

2

3

VALUE

Value means how dark or light a fabric is compared to the fabrics around it. Determine the value of fabrics by squinting at them or by looking at them through the Ruby Beholder® from That Patchwork Place.

In some of the quilt patterns in this book, we call for fabric of a certain value, but feel free to experiment with color and value placement.

Fabric Selection Recipe

Choose favorite fabrics and colors.

Add light, medium, and dark values

of those fabric colors.

Mix in "magic" fabrics.

Add a pinch of "electric" fabric, twice.

Blend well;

do not overmix.

Serves 1 or more

Little Quilts.

YARDAGE AMOUNTS

It is difficult to give exact yardage amounts for Little Quilts, because much of the charm of Little Quilts comes from the use of many fabrics in small quantities. If you already have a fabric collection, you may only need to add a few "magic" fabrics or fabric of a certain value. If you are a new quiltmaker, or if you have a limited fabric collection, we suggest that you purchase twenty-five to fifty fat quarters (18" x 22") of assorted fabrics. Be sure to include an ample supply of the "magic" fabrics and some "electric" ones too. From this supply you will be able to make lots of Little Quilts.

Purchase what your budget allows, but add to your collection continuously. Don't just buy fabrics for a specific project. Go on a fabric shopping "mission," searching for a particular style or color, such as plaids, darks, greens, and so on. Trade fabric with your quilting friends to add variety to your collection. Substitute similar fabrics for a project if you run out of one print. Look at the color photographs of our quilts to see examples of fabric variety.

The fabric requirements listed for the projects in this book are approximate. *Cut borders and sashing strips on the lengthwise grain whenever possible.* All fabric requirements are based on this cutting direction, except for bindings, which are cut across the grain. You may cut borders across the grain if you choose.

BATTING

An important ingredient in the Little Quilts look is the batting. Use thin batting when making these quilts. You can split traditional batting by carefully pulling it apart. Cotton batting is a good choice, but it requires more quilting than polyester or polyester-cotton blends. The finished quilt should lie flat.

OTHER SUPPLIES

In order to assemble your Little Quilt, you need the following basic supplies.
★ Neutral color thread for sewing, such as tan or gray. (Change the needle on your sewing machine frequently.)
★ Quilting thread in ecru, tan, or black.
★ Rotary cutter, cutting mat, and rulers for cutting strips and other pieces.
★ About 1½ yards of fleece for a great design wall (page 12).
★ Miscellaneous supplies include an iron, template plastic, scissors, needles, thimble, pencils, pins, a fine-tip permanent-ink pen (black), polyester fiberfill, embroidery floss, old buttons, and a reducing glass (optional). You can substitute a pair of binoculars, used the wrong way around, for the reducing glass.

More Strips!

Cut your leftover fabric into strips and store them, sorted by size, in baskets where they will be ready for your next project. We cut and save strips in the following widths:

1¼"	2"
1½"	2¼"
1¾"	

When we cut fabric for any project, we also cut strips for our baskets. These strips are useful for making blocks or for auditioning color for sashing. We often use strips from the basket as "coping" strips to make blocks fit together when we make a scrap quilt. You can even place templates on strips, then cut the required pattern pieces. Whenever possible, cut strips on the lengthwise grain of the fabric.

For the projects in this book, we have used the strip sizes suggested above. Try cutting strips from Amish solids and in wider widths.

The Design Wall

A design wall made of cotton flannel or polyester fleece is invaluable when constructing a quilt of any size, especially a Little Quilt. You can arrange blocks on the wall and then stand back to see how they look. It's easy to audition borders for your project on the wall too.

To make a design wall, purchase 1½ yards of flannel or fleece. Tack or tape the fleece to a wall. If you do not have a spare wall, cover a large piece of plywood or foam-core board (from the art supply store). You can easily store this board when it is not in use.

A reducing glass, which is the reverse of a magnifying glass, also helps you see what your quilt will look like from a distance. You can buy one at your local quilt shop or art supply store.

A design wall, with the blocks and other pieces ready to design a Little Quilt.

Let's Celebrate!

It's somebody's birthday! On the wall are the Alphabet Crib Quilt *(left) and the antique* Ninepatch Doll Quilt *(right). The bears are sitting on* Candy Baskets, *and little pillows and party favors (here's another way to use those blocks!) decorate the table.*

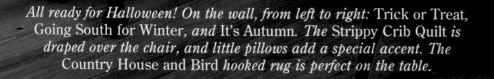

All ready for Halloween! On the wall, from left to right: Trick or Treat, Going South for Winter, *and* It's Autumn. *The* Strippy Crib Quilt *is draped over the chair, and little pillows add a special accent. The* Country House and Bird *hooked rug is perfect on the table.*

It's holiday time! Displayed on the wall, from left to right, are Pine Trees *and* Mr. Snowman. Open Me First! *decorates the table, along with little pillows. The* Mr. Snowman *rug adorns the bench behind the table, and the antique* Ninepatch Doll Quilt *is draped over the chair.*

A patriotic celebration! America *hanging over the fireplace
sets the theme;* The Country House and Bird *rug hangs under the mantel.
A heart quilt (see* Little Quilts, All Through The House*) and an antique
doll quilt (no pattern given) decorate the table and chair.
Lots of little flags and pillows complete the theme.*

The first day of school. Little Amish Houses hangs on the wall. On the top row of the drying rack, from left to right: an antique Tumbling Blocks doll quilt, Sawtooth Doll Quilt, and Ninepatch Doll Quilt. An antique crazy quilt (no pattern) hangs with them. Underneath are several doll quilts, including some made from antique blocks. Another antique doll quilt (no pattern) covers the bed, and the Hearts and Stars hooked rug is just right for little bear feet.

WELCOME
FRIENDS

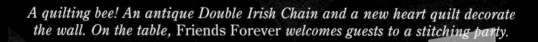

A quilting bee! An antique Double Irish Chain and a new heart quilt decorate the wall. On the table, Friends Forever *welcomes guests to a stitching party.*

QUILTS

You Are Special *sets the tone for this birthday party. On the wall, from left to right:* Strippy Crib Quilt, Little Amish Houses, *and an* Amish Fourpatch. *The antique* Sawtooth Doll Quilt *props up a bear.*

General Directions

Little Quilts are fun and quick to make. We have included instructions for rotary cutting and machine piecing, as well as for hand piecing. You can use the templates on pages 78–87 if you wish to use traditional methods to make the blocks. If you use rotary-cutting methods, compare rotary-cut pieces to the templates to check for accuracy. All measurements include ¼"-wide seam allowances unless otherwise noted.

HAND PIECING

Years ago, many quilters had only basic supplies with which to practice their craft: leftover fabric or pieces from worn clothing, thread and needle, pins, and a marking pencil. They made cutting templates from tin or from cardboard that was recycled from a gift or cereal box. Patterns were passed from friend to friend.

Quiltmakers sewed a few pieces together as time allowed. These bits and pieces added up, and soon they had a finished quilt top. Quilters of the past did appliqué too, but they saved it for sunny days when it was easier to see, or for when their disposition was good.

We do things differently today. New tools and sewing machines make quiltmaking easier and faster. Fabrics are plentiful and new gadgets are continually invented to speed up every step of the process.

In this hurry-up world, many of us still crave time to work quietly by hand. Hand piecing is like sewing a fabric puzzle, and accuracy is important for success. Trace the hand-piecing templates on plastic, following the dashed lines on the inside of the templates, *not* the outer solid line. Mark the grain line. Place the template on the wrong side of the fabric, paying attention to the fabric grain line, and trace around it with a sharp pencil. This is the sewing line. Cut ¼" beyond this line to add the seam allowance.

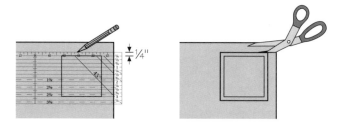

Everything you need to piece by hand.

Arrange the pieces, right sides up. Pin them to a square of muslin to keep them in order.

Sew small units together to make larger ones; follow the piecing diagrams for the quilt you are making. Pin pieces together, matching seam lines. Sew on the lines with a small running stitch, and check to make sure you are stitching on the lines of both pieces. Sew only on the lines; seam allowances must remain free.

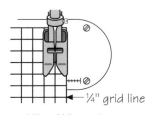

— Stitching line

Use regular sewing thread in a matching color, or use a neutral shade such as gray or tan. Take an occasional backstitch while sewing to strengthen the seam. Hand-pieced quilt blocks have a softer feel because there is less thread along the seam lines; as a result, quilting is generally easier.

Trim the seams to ⅛" after sewing each one. When the block is complete, press it well, pressing seams toward the darker fabric whenever possible.

ROTARY CUTTING

With a rotary cutter, acrylic ruler, and mat, you can accurately cut several layers of fabric at one time. These tools are invaluable when making multi-fabric quilts, whether you plan to piece by hand or machine. You can use the rotary cutter to cut strips for many of the projects in this book. The Bias Square®, a rotary ruler, is useful for squaring up blocks for Little Quilts.

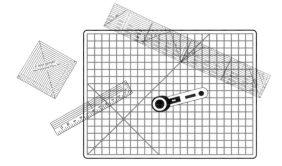

MACHINE PIECING

What we think is a ¼"-wide seam is often too wide or too narrow. Any variation in a ¼"-wide seam allowance will affect the size of your block. Use a ruler, or graph paper with a ¼" grid, to check this measurement on your machine and determine a guide for your sewing. Place a piece of masking tape on the throat plate of the machine to mark your "spot."

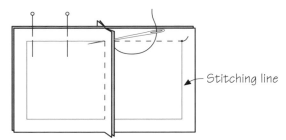

← ¼" grid line	

Use ¼" or ⅛" graph paper to locate a new seam guide.

Put masking tape in front of needle along edge of graph paper to guide fabric.

Change your needle frequently, and use ten to twelve stitches per inch. Backstitching is not necessary, since seams will cross each other. Chain piecing saves both time and thread.

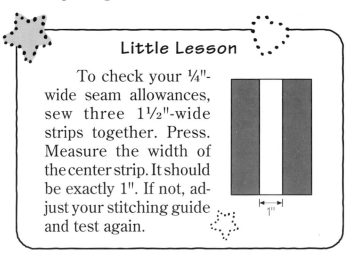

Little Lesson

To check your ¼"-wide seam allowances, sew three 1½"-wide strips together. Press. Measure the width of the center strip. It should be exactly 1". If not, adjust your stitching guide and test again.

├ 1" ┤

PRESSING

It is important to press seams as you sew them. This helps with matching seams and also helps to ensure that the finished block will be the correct size. Pull your ironing board close to your machine. If you need the exercise, place it across the room so you are forced to move!

After sewing strips together by machine, press the seams flat while they are closed before pressing them to one side. This relaxes and sets the stitching and keeps the strips straight. Press seams in one direction, toward the darker fabric.

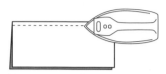

Press seam after sewing, before pressing one way or the other.

Press seam open by opening the pieces with the iron.

HAND APPLIQUÉ

Templates for hand-appliqué pieces do not include seam allowances. Place the template right side up on the right side of the fabric and trace around it. Cut ⅛" to ¼" from this line. Turn under the seam allowance and finger-press. Baste close to the edge to hold the seam allowance in place.

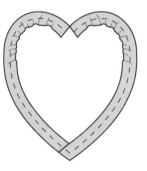

Clip only where necessary. Pin the pieces in place, noting where one piece may overlap another. A seam allowance that is overlapped by another piece need not be basted under. A dotted line indicates overlapped areas on pattern pieces.

Do not turn under and baste area under hat.

Appliqué with a single thread in a color that matches the appliqué piece. Sew the piece in place with an appliqué stitch. A running stitch will appear on the back.

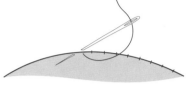
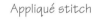

Appliqué stitch

Back view

The needle-turn method works well for simple shapes, such as hearts. Baste the shape to the background fabric about ⅛" inside the drawn line. Use the needle to turn the seam allowance under as you sew around the appliqué. Trim away excess seam allowance as you sew.

FUSIBLE APPLIQUÉ

Many fusing products are available for applying one piece of fabric to another. You can use this method of "quick" appliqué to save time. Fabrics do stiffen after application, so choose a light-weight web. Follow the manufacturer's directions for the product you select. *You must reverse the templates when you draw them onto the paper side of the fusible web.* Do not add seam allowances to the appliqué pieces when using the fusible appliqué method.

ALPHABET APPLIQUÉ

Personalize your quilts! Create your own designs with fabric letters embellished with the buttonhole stitch.

1. Make plastic templates of the letters of the alphabet (pages 86–87). If necessary, mark the top and bottom edges of the letters to avoid placing them upside down or backward (*C* and *S*, for example).
2. Fuse web to the fabric as desired.
3. Place the templates right side down on the paper side of the fused fabric, trace around them, and cut them out carefully.

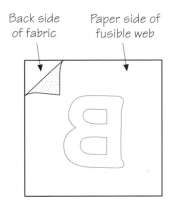

Back side of fabric   Paper side of fusible web

4. Prepare 5½" x 5½" background squares or a strip of background fabric.
5. Peel the paper backing from the letters. Try several arrangements before fusing them on the background.

6. Fuse the letters to the background fabric.
7. Using two strands of embroidery floss, buttonhole-stitch the edges, following the directions in the box at right.

The Buttonhole Stitch

Many quilts in this book have appliqué pieces embellished with the buttonhole stitch. This stitch defines shapes and gives an old-fashioned look to a quilt. You can use a paper-backed fusible web to fuse the appliqué shapes in place. Add the buttonhole-stitch embellishment *before* assembling blocks or adding borders.

1. Use two strands of embroidery floss, about 20" long, and a sharp embroidery needle.
2. Begin with a knot on the back and end by weaving a small amount of thread into the previous stitches on the back of the work. This will secure the end.
3. Bring the needle out at the edge of the piece and work from left to right.
4. Move the needle to the right and take a stitch at a 90° angle to the edge of the fabric. Keep the thread under the needle and bring the needle out at the edge of the appliqué.
5. Turn corners as shown.

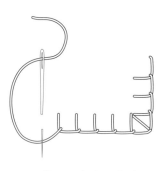

Buttonhole stitch

You can use the buttonhole stitch available on some sewing machines to save time. Practice turning corners and using various stitch widths and threads on scraps of fabric first.

QUILT FINISHING

After you have assembled the Little Quilt top, it's time to add borders, layer with batting and backing, then quilt and bind.

Adding Borders

Measure your quilt through the center to determine the length of the borders. Cut border strips to that measurement.

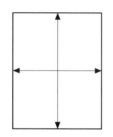

Quilts that have pieced borders, such as "You are Special" on page 35 and "America" on page 64 must be sewn accurately in order to fit together as planned.

Quilting

Quilting will slightly reduce the size of your finished quilt top. Mark quilting lines lightly with an ordinary pencil, washable fabric marker, or white pencil. Masking tape in different widths is also helpful for marking quilting lines. Cut backing and batting a few inches larger than the quilt top all the way around. Layer backing, batting, and quilt top; then baste layers together.

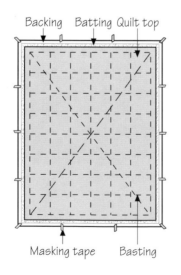

Backing Batting Quilt top

Masking tape   Basting

To quilt by hand:

1. Tie a single knot in the end of an 18" length of quilting thread.
2. Insert the needle in the top layer of the quilt about ½" from where you want to start quilting. Quilt from the center out to the edges and use a quilting hoop to hold the work whenever possible. Slide the needle through the batting and bring it out on the marked quilting line. Gently tug on the thread until the knot pops through the fabric, burying the knot in the batting.
3. Make small, even stitches through all layers, following your marked quilting lines.
4. To end your stitches, make a single knot about ¼" from the quilt top. Take the next stitch but keep the needle between the layers of fabric. Bring the needle out ½" from your last stitch and tug on the knot until it pops into the batting. Clip the thread and work it back into the sandwich.

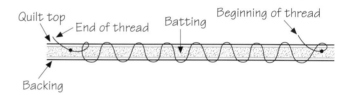

Quilt top   End of thread   Batting   Beginning of thread

Backing

Many of the projects presented in this book are quilted "in-the-ditch," which means to quilt in the seam line of the block or patchwork shape. Quilt on the side opposite the seam allowances. This makes the quilting easier because there are fewer layers through which to stitch.

Binding

1. Trim away excess batting and backing.
2. Cut 1¼"- to 1½"-wide strips across the width of the fabric (crosswise grain), or use strips from your basket. Join enough strips to go around the quilt, plus 4" to 5" extra.
3. Place binding on the quilt top with right sides together and raw edges even. Fold ½" of the binding back and pin.
4. Place pins along one side at a time and sew through all layers, using a ¼"-wide seam

allowance. Stop stitching ¼" from the corner; backstitch. Clip threads and remove the piece from the machine. Fold the binding straight up, then straight down parallel to the next edge. Stitch from edge as shown.

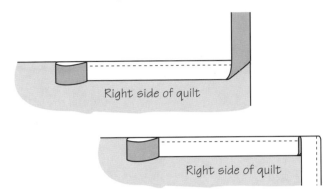

Repeat for each corner. When you reach the starting point, sew the end across the beginning fold. Cut off excess binding. Bring the raw edge over to the back, fold under ¼", and blindstitch in place, covering the machine stitching. Tuck corners to form a miter.

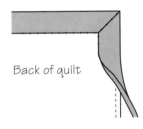

LABELING YOUR LITTLE QUILT

Make a Little Quilt label for your finished quilt. Cut a piece of muslin approximately 4" x 5" and iron it onto the shiny side of a piece of freezer paper to provide a firm surface for writing. Place the muslin piece over the label design on page 85 and trace carefully, using a fine-point permanent-ink pen. Use a pen with a contrasting ink color to fill in the information. Remove the freezer paper after you finish writing. Trim away any excess muslin. Turn under a ¼"-wide allowance all around and carefully slipstitch the label to the back of the quilt, making sure the needle doesn't go through to the front.

HANGING LITTLE QUILTS

★ Sew decorative wire hangers to the top of the quilt; then hang on tiny nails.
★ Use straight pins. Push them through the corners of the quilt into the wall.
★ Attach two small, rust-proof safety pins to the back of the quilt, close to the top; then hang on tiny nails.
★ Attach a fabric "sleeve" to the back and insert a strip of lattice with holes in it for hanging on small nails.
★ Frame your Little Quilt.

TEA DYEING

Use a tea bath to "age" your quilt. When you finish the quilt, place it in the tea solution. This makes for a nervous moment, but we haven't seen a Little Quilt yet that didn't benefit from this "aging" process. If you prefer not to tea dye, a gentle washing will also soften the look.

Our Tea Dyeing Recipe

2 quarts *hot* tap water in a large bowl
6 to 8 tea bags
(Double this recipe for crib quilts.)

Steep tea bags in hot water for 15 minutes. Remove tea bags. Add the quilt and soak it in the tea solution for 15 to 30 minutes. Rinse the quilt in cool water. Squeeze out excess water. Lay flat to dry. Press the quilt to reshape.

EMBELLISHING WITH BUTTONS

Old buttons add charm to Little Quilts. Sew buttons on after the quilt has been completed, using embroidery floss. No specific number of buttons is required; just scatter them at random on the quilt and sew in place.

Shortcuts

The patchwork blocks used in Little Quilts are simple to construct. Some of the shortcuts described in this section will make your sewing even easier and faster.

HALF-SQUARE TRIANGLES

Rotary-cutting and machine-piecing blocks made of two right-angle triangles is a snap. Determine the finished size of the short side of the triangle needed. Add $\frac{7}{8}$" to this measurement. Cut a square this size, then cut it once diagonally for two triangles. Sew pairs of triangles together to make a half-square triangle block, or use them for corner triangles on diagonally set quilts.

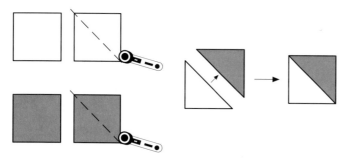

QUARTER-SQUARE TRIANGLES

Use these pieces for side setting triangles on diagonally set quilts. The straight of grain is on the outside or long edge of the triangle. To cut these pieces without a template, cut a square that is $1\frac{1}{4}$" larger than the finished long side of the triangle. Cut the square twice diagonally for four triangles.

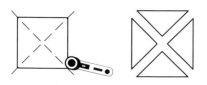

SIMPLE FOUR PATCH BLOCKS

Choose pieces from your basket of $2\frac{1}{4}$"-wide strips and sew them together in pairs. Use many short strips for variety. Press the seams toward the darker fabric in each strip-pieced unit. Crosscut the sewn strips into sections the same width as the strip. Join two sections to form the Four Patch block.

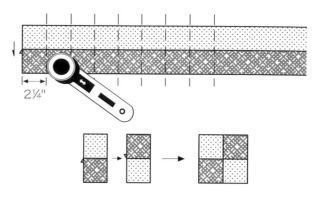

SCRAPPY NINEPATCH BLOCKS

Using pieces from your basket of $1\frac{1}{4}$"-wide strips, sew the strips together in pairs. Choose many short strips for variety. Press the seams flat along the stitching line, then press the seam to one side. Add a third strip and press toward the same side. Crosscut the strip-pieced units into segments the same width as the strips.

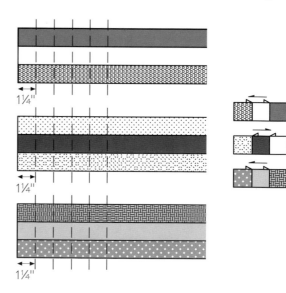

FLYING GEESE

These little geese will just fly from your machine into a quilt! Use pieces from your basket of 1¾" strips. For each unit cut:

1 rectangle of dark fabric, 1¾" x 3";

2 squares of light fabric, each 1¾" x 1¾".

1. Draw a diagonal line from corner to corner on the wrong side of the light squares.

2. Place a square on one end of the rectangle, right sides together. Sew on the marked line. Trim the corner triangle, leaving a small seam allowance. Do not trim away the corner of the rectangle. Press the triangle toward the corner.

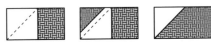

3. Place the second square on the opposite end of the rectangle, with the marked line as shown. Sew, trim, and press.

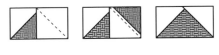

Note

When sewing Flying Geese blocks together, place the blocks with right sides together and stitch with the point of the large triangle on top. Sew a "thread's width" away from the point of the triangle where the seams cross.

Little Tip

1. Chain-piece the sections, sewing a square to one end of the rectangle.

2. Cut the units apart, trim the triangle, and press. Chain-piece the other side in the same manner. Make more than you need so you can use them in other projects.

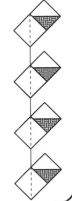

Little Pillows

Fill a basket with these pillows, or put one in a child's chair! Use leftover blocks and strips and let your imagination run wild. Little pillows make great hostess gifts and party favors.

OPTIONS

Choose a quilt block; then complete it in one of the following ways.

★ Frame a block with precut strips. Sew the strips to the sides of the block first, then to the top and bottom.

★ Add a narrow framing strip to a block; then add a wider border. Sew strips to the sides of the block first, then to the top and bottom.

★ Sew leftover patchwork strips and squares around a block.

★ Use corner triangles to put a block on point.

Construction

1. Layer the backing, batting, and pillow top; baste.

2. Quilt the pillow top as desired. Simple quilting is sufficient.

3. Baste around the edges of the quilted pillow top to hold the layers together.

4. Add button embellishments.

5. Place the pillow top and back right sides together. Sew ¼" from the raw edges, leaving a 2"-long opening for stuffing. Turn the pillowcase right side out and stuff firmly. Blindstitch the opening closed.

The Little Blocks

Half-Square Triangle
Finished Size: 1½"
Template: N

Flying Geese
Finished Size: 1¼" x 2½"
Templates: FF, Z

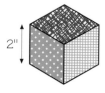

Tumbling Block
Finished Side Measurement: 2"
Template: JJ

Strippy Four Patch
Finished Size: 3½"
Template: GG

Heart
Finished Size: 5"
Templates: Y, QQ

Alphabet Blocks
Finished Size: 5"
Templates: Y, Letters

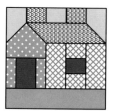

Star
Finished Size: 5"
Templates: Y, TT

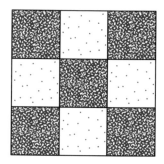

Large Ninepatch
Finished Size: 9"
Template: D

Small Ninepatch
Finished Size: 2¼"
Template: O

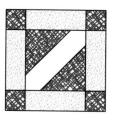

Signature Block
Finished Size: 5"
Templates: L, P, AA, BB

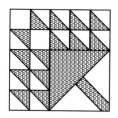

House
Finished Size: 5"
Templates: E, F, G, H, I, J, K, M

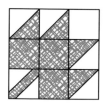

Pine Tree
Finished Size: 5"
Templates: L, U, B

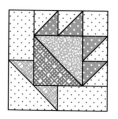

Basket
Finished Size: 5"
Templates: CC, DD, EE, FF

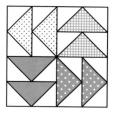

Dutchman's Puzzle
Finished Size: 5"
Templates: FF, Z

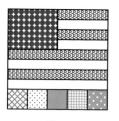

Flag
Finished Size: 5"
Templates: OO, PP, NN, L

Maple Leaf
Finished Size: 4½"
Templates: A, N

Friends Forever

Finished Quilt Size: 18½" x 23½"

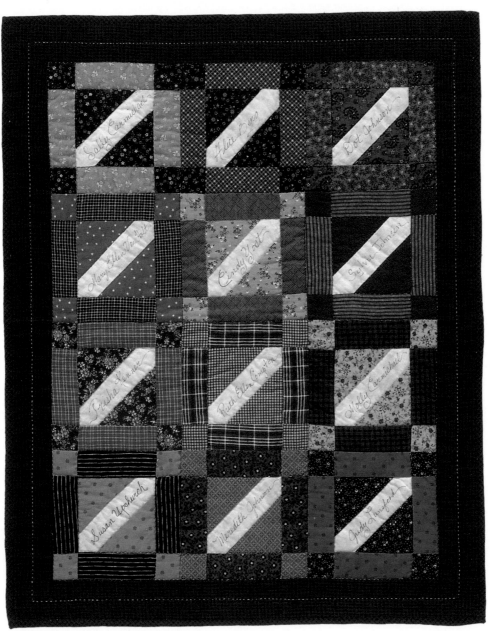

Friends Forever *by Little Quilts, 1993, Marietta, Georgia, 18½" x 23½". Everyone has a special way to collect memories. It is only natural that a quilter would choose fabric.*

Signature Block
Finished Size: 5"
Templates: L, P, AA, BB

Materials: 44"-wide fabric

⅛ yd. each of 24 different fabrics
in assorted colors for the blocks
⅛ yd. muslin for the signature strips
⅝ yd. red for border
¼ yd. for binding
⅝ yd. for backing
21" x 26" piece of thin batting

Rotary Cutting

If you prefer to hand piece, see "Template Cutting" above right. Cut the pieces from 1½"-wide precut strips.

1. From each of 12 assorted fabrics, cut 4 squares, each 1½" x 1½". From each of the same 12 fabrics, cut 1 square, 3⅛" x 3⅛". Crosscut each of the large squares once diagonally to yield a total of 24 triangles.
2. From each of the 12 remaining fabrics, cut 4 rectangles, each 1½" x 3½".
3. From muslin, cut 2 strips, 1⅝" x 42". From the strips, cut 12 pieces (Template BB).
4. To assemble the blocks and complete the quilt top, see the remaining directions, beginning with "Block Assembly" at right.

Template Cutting

Use Templates L, P, AA, and BB on pages 78, 79 and 81.

1. From each of 12 assorted fabrics, cut 4 squares (Template L), and 2 triangles (Template P), for a total of 48 squares and 24 triangles.
2. From each of the 12 remaining fabrics, cut 4 rectangles (Template AA), for a total of 48 rectangles.
3. From muslin, cut 12 pieces (Template BB).

Block Assembly

1. Sew matching triangles to opposite sides of each muslin center strip (piece BB). Press the seams toward the triangles.

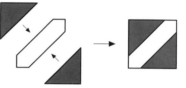

2. Sew matching rectangles (piece AA) to each side of the center square. Press the seams toward the rectangles.

3. Sew a small square (piece L) to each end of 2 matching rectangles. Press the seams toward the rectangles.

4. Complete each block as shown.

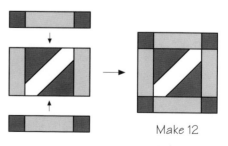

Make 12

5. Sign the blocks with a permanent-ink pen before assembling the quilt top.

Quilt Top Assembly

1. Arrange the blocks as shown below.
2. Stitch the blocks together in rows. Press seams in opposite directions from row to row.
3. Sew the rows together, matching seams.
4. Measure the quilt top for borders as described in "Adding Borders" on page 24. From the red fabric, cut 2 strips, each 2" wide by the length of your quilt top. Sew the strips to opposite sides of the quilt top and press the seams toward the border.
5. From the red fabric, cut 2 strips, each 2" wide by the width of your quilt top, including the side borders. Sew the strips to the top and bottom edges of the quilt top and press the seams toward the borders as shown.

Quilt Finishing

Refer to "Quilt Finishing" on pages 24–25.

1. Layer the quilt top with batting and backing; baste. Quilt as desired.

☼ Suggestion

Quilt the Signature blocks in-the-ditch. Quilt a straight line down the center of the border, approximately ¾" from the seam.

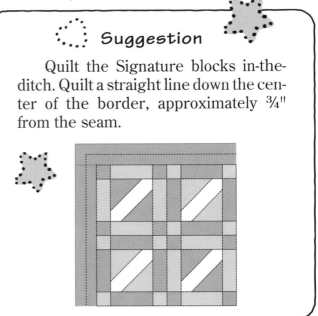

2. Bind the edges of the quilt.
3. Tea dye if desired.
4. Press the quilt.

Candy Baskets

Finished Quilt Size: 29½" x 29½"

Candy Baskets *by Little Quilts, 1994, Marietta, Georgia, 29½" x 29½".*
What party is complete without little baskets filled with goodies? Quilted by Janet Rawls.

Basket
Finished Size: 5"
Templates: CC, DD, EE, FF

Materials: 44"-wide fabric

¾ yd. total assorted medium and
light prints for the blocks
¾ yd. pink for inner border
1 yd. for outer border
¼ yd. for binding
1 yd. for backing
34" x 34" piece of thin batting

Rotary Cutting

If you prefer to hand piece, see "Template Cutting" at right. Letters refer to placement for block assembly.

1. From the assorted medium prints, cut:
   27 squares, each 2⅛" x 2⅛". Cut each square once diagonally for 54 triangles, 6 for each block (FF).
   9 squares, each 3⅜" x 3⅜". Cut each square once diagonally for 18 triangles, 2 for each block (EE).
2. From the assorted light prints, cut:
   9 squares, each 1¾" x 1¾" (CC).
   18 squares, each 2⅛" x 2⅛". Cut each square once diagonally for a total of 36 triangles, 4 for each block (FF).
   5 squares, each 3⅜" x 3⅜". Cut each square once diagonally for 10 triangles, one for each block and 1 extra (EE).
   18 rectangles, each 1¾" x 3", 2 for each block (DD).
   18 squares, each 4⅜" x 4⅜". Cut each square twice diagonally for 36 triangles, 4 for each block. Reserve for "Block Assembly," step 3.
3. See "Block Assembly" at right to construct the blocks.

Template Cutting

Use Templates CC, DD, EE, FF, and X on pages 80–81.

1. From the assorted medium prints, cut:
   18 triangles (Template EE), 2 for each block;
   54 triangles (Template FF), 6 for each block.
2. From the assorted light prints, cut:
   36 triangles (Template FF), 4 for each block;
   9 triangles (Template EE), 1 for each block;
   9 squares (Template CC), 1 for each block;
   18 rectangles (Template DD), 2 for each block;
   36 triangles (Template X), 4 for each block.
   Reserve for "Block Assembly," step 3.

Block Assembly

1. Arrange the pieces for each of the 9 blocks.

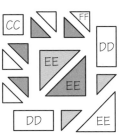

2. Assemble each Basket block in the order shown below. Press the seams toward the darker color whenever possible.

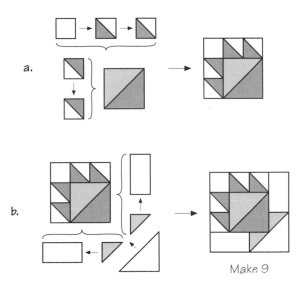

Make 9

3. Sew a reserved triangle to opposite sides of each block, then to the remaining sides. For each block, choose triangles that are different fabrics but similar colors. Press the seams toward the triangles.

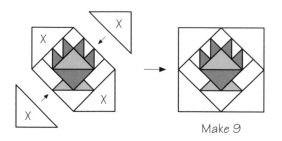

Make 9

Quilt Top Assembly

1. Arrange blocks in 3 rows of 3 blocks each.
2. Sew the blocks together in rows; press the seams in opposite directions from row to row.
3. Sew the rows together, matching seams carefully.
4. Measure the quilt top for borders as described in "Adding Borders" on page 24. From the pink fabric, cut 2 strips, each 1½" wide by the length of the quilt top. Sew the strips to opposite sides of the quilt top and press the seams, and all remaining border seams, toward the border.
5. From the pink fabric, cut 2 strips, each 1½" wide by the width of the quilt top, including the side borders. Sew the strips to the top and bottom edges of the quilt top.
6. From outer border fabric, cut 2 strips, each 3½" wide by the length of the quilt top. Sew to opposite sides of the quilt top.
7. From the outer border fabric, cut 2 strips, each 3½" wide by the width of the quilt top, including the side borders. Sew the strips to the top and bottom edges of the quilt top.

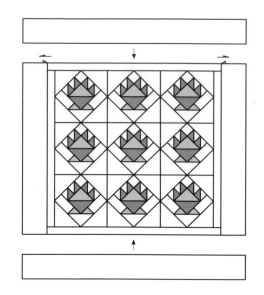

Quilt Finishing

Refer to "Quilt Finishing" on pages 24–25.
1. Layer the quilt top with batting and backing; baste. Quilt as desired.

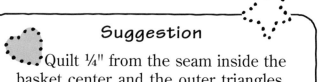

Suggestion

Quilt ¼" from the seam inside the basket center and the outer triangles. Quilt in-the-ditch in the other areas. Quilt a line ½" inside the inner border. Draw a wavy line to resemble party streamers in the outer border; quilt along the line.

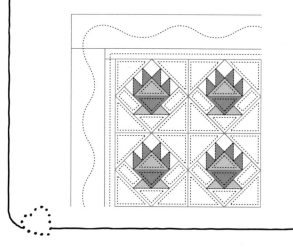

2. Bind the edges of the quilt.
3. Tea dye if desired.
4. Press the quilt.

You Are Special

Finished Quilt Size: 38" x 38"

You Are Special *by Little Quilts, 1994, Marietta, Georgia, 38" x 38". Let someone know how you feel!*

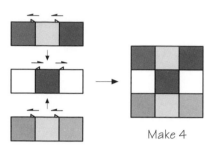

Flying Geese
Finished Size: 1¼" x 2½"
Templates: FF, Z

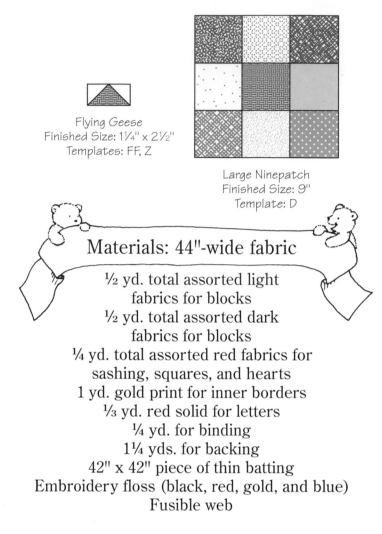

Large Ninepatch
Finished Size: 9"
Template: D

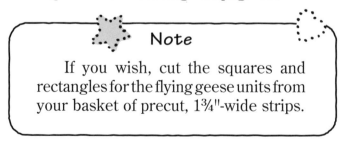

Materials: 44"-wide fabric

½ yd. total assorted light
fabrics for blocks
½ yd. total assorted dark
fabrics for blocks
¼ yd. total assorted red fabrics for
sashing, squares, and hearts
1 yd. gold print for inner borders
⅓ yd. red solid for letters
¼ yd. for binding
1¼ yds. for backing
42" x 42" piece of thin batting
Embroidery floss (black, red, gold, and blue)
Fusible web

Rotary Cutting and Machine Piecing

If you prefer to hand piece, see "Template Cutting and Hand Piecing" on page 37.

Note

If you wish, cut the squares and rectangles for the flying geese units from your basket of precut, 1¾"-wide strips.

1. From the assorted light and dark fabrics, cut 36 squares, each 3½" x 3½", for the Ninepatch blocks.

2. Arrange the squares in 3 rows of 3 squares each for a total of 4 blocks. Sew the squares together in rows, pressing the seams in opposite directions from row to row. Sew the rows together to make each block.

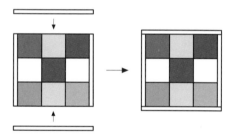

Make 4

3. From the assorted red fabrics, cut 8 strips, each 1" x 9½", and 8 strips, each 1" x 10½". Sew a short strip to opposite sides of each Ninepatch block. Press the seams toward the strips. Add a long strip to the top and bottom edge of each block.

4. From the assorted red fabrics, cut 5 squares, each 3" x 3", for the center and outer corner squares. Set aside.

5. From the assorted dark fabrics, cut 136 rectangles, each 1¾" x 3", for the flying geese units.

6. From the assorted light fabrics, cut 272 squares, each 1¾" x 1¾", for the flying geese units.

7. Make 136 flying geese units, referring to "Flying Geese" on page 27.

8. To complete the quilt top, see the remaining assembly directions, beginning with "Appliqué" on page 37.

Template Cutting and Hand Piecing

Use Templates D, FF, MM, and Z on pages 78, 81, and 82.

1. From the assorted light and dark fabrics, cut 36 squares (Template D) for the Ninepatch blocks.
2. Arrange the squares and sew them together as directed in step 2 of "Rotary Cutting and Machine Piecing" above.
3. From the assorted red fabrics, cut 8 strips, each 1" x 9½", and 8 strips, each 1" x 10½". Sew a short strip to opposite sides of each Ninepatch block. Press the seams toward the strips. Add a long strip to the top and bottom edge of each block.
4. From the assorted red fabrics, cut 5 squares (Template MM) for the center and outer corner squares. Set aside.
5. From the assorted dark fabrics, cut 136 triangles (Template Z) for the flying geese units.
6. From the assorted light fabrics, cut 272 triangles (Template FF) for the flying geese units.
7. Sew a light triangle to each side of each dark triangle as shown to make 136 flying geese units.

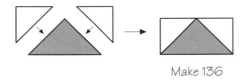

Make 136

Appliqué

Use Heart Template QQ on page 80, Star Template TT on page 79, and the Alphabet templates on pages 86–87.

1. From the assorted red fabrics, cut 7 stars and 5 hearts.
2. Arrange the hearts and stars on the Ninepatch blocks, referring to the quilt photo on page 35 for placement ideas.
3. Appliqué the hearts and stars in place. See "Hand Appliqué" on page 22.
4. Buttonhole-stitch (page 23) around the edges of the hearts and stars.

5. From the gold print, cut 2 strips, each 5½" x 23", for the side borders, and 2 strips, each 5½" x 33", for the top and bottom borders.
6. Using the necessary alphabet templates to spell "You Are Special," cut 2 of each piece from the red solid.
7. Referring to the quilt photo, arrange the letters for "Special" on each of the short gold border strips and the letters for "You Are" on the longer border strips.
8. Appliqué the letters in place, referring to "Alphabet Appliqué" on page 23. Buttonhole-stitch around the edges of the letters. Set aside the completed borders.

Quilt Top Assembly

Little Tip

Pay careful attention to sewing accurate ¼"-wide seams to ensure that the pieces fit together. To avoid distortion, press the flying geese strips carefully. Do not stretch them out of shape.

1. Join 8 flying geese units to form a strip, making sure that all units point in the same direction. Repeat to make a total of 4 flying geese strips that each measure 10½" long. If necessary, adjust the length of individual strips by taking in or letting out seams.

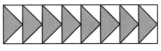

Make 4

2. Use the remaining flying geese units to make 8 strips, each containing 13 units. Set these aside for the outer borders.

Make 8

3. Arrange the Ninepatch blocks, short flying geese strips, and one 3" x 3" red square as shown, making sure that the flying geese all point toward the red center square.

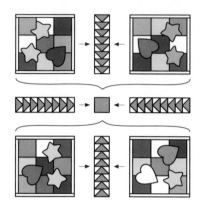

4. Sew the units together in 3 rows, pressing all seams away from the flying geese strips.
5. Sew the short gold border strips to opposite sides of the quilt top; then sew the long strips to the top and bottom edges. Press the seams toward the borders. When attaching the borders, be sure that the tops of the letters are toward the center of the quilt top.
6. Sew 2 of the 13-unit flying geese strips together, making sure that they point toward the outer ends of the strip. Repeat to make a total of 4 strips, each 33" long. If necessary, adjust seams to make the outer borders the correct length.

Make 4

Add a 3" x 3" red corner square to opposite ends of 2 of these strips.

Make 2

7. Sew the flying geese border strips to opposite sides of the quilt top and press the seams toward the gold border. Add the border strips with red corner squares to the top and bottom edges of the quilt top.

Quilt Finishing

Refer to "Quilt Finishing" on pages 24–25.
1. Layer the quilt top with batting and backing; baste. Quilt as desired.

Suggestion

Quilt around the letters and appliqué shapes. Quilt in-the-ditch in the red strips around the Ninepatch blocks and in the flying geese. Quilt a line ¼" from the seam inside the appliqué border. Quilt a diagonal square in the corners and in the center square.

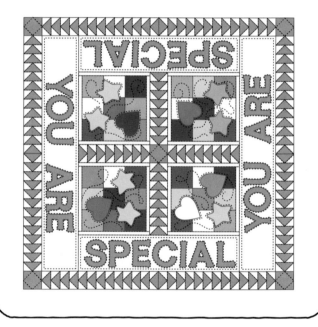

2. Bind the edges of the quilt.
3. Tea dye if desired.
4. Press the quilt.

Sunshine, flowers, falling leaves, and snow;
Mother Nature is constantly redecorating!
Everyone has a favorite season to celebrate.

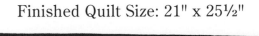

It's Autumn

Finished Quilt Size: 21" x 25½"

It's Autumn *by Little Quilts, 1994, Marietta, Georgia, 21" x 25½".*
There's a chill in the air and the leaves have begun to turn color and toss in the wind.

Maple Leaf
Finished Size: 4½"
Templates: A, N

Materials: 44"-wide fabric

⅜ yd. total assorted blacks
for background
⅛ yd. total assorted golds for leaves
⅛ yd. total assorted reds for leaves
⅛ yd. total assorted greens for leaves
⅛ yd. total assorted rusts for leaves
¾ yd. brown for border
¼ yd. for binding
¾ yd. for backing
24" x 29" piece of thin batting

Cutting

Rotary-cut the following pieces, or if you prefer to hand-piece, use Templates A and N on pages 78–79.

1. From the black fabrics, cut:
   48 triangles (Template N). Or rotary-cut 24 squares, each 2⅜" x 2⅜"; cut the squares once diagonally for a total of 48 half-square triangles.
   24 squares (Template A), or rotary-cut 24 squares, each 2" x 2".

2. From the assorted gold, red, green, and rust fabrics, cut:
   48 half-square triangles (Template N), or rotary-cut 24 squares, each 2⅜" x 2⅜"; cut the squares once diagonally for a total of 48 half-square triangles.
   36 squares (Template A), or rotary-cut 36 squares, each 2" x 2".
   12 bias strips, each 1" x 2¾", for the stems.

Block Assembly

1. To make the stems, fold each of the 12 bias strips as shown and press.

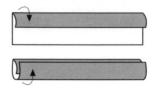

2. Position each stem on a 2" x 2" brown background square and appliqué (page 22) using matching thread.

Make 12

3. Sew each background triangle to a leaf triangle. Press the seam toward the darker triangle.

Make 48

4. Arrange the half-square triangle units, remaining background squares, leaf squares, and the stem squares to make 12 blocks.

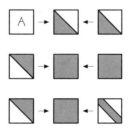

5. Sew the units together in rows, pressing the seams in opposite directions; then join the rows to complete each block.

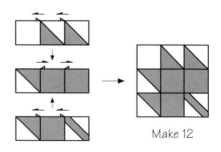

Make 12

Quilt Top Assembly

1. Arrange the Leaf blocks so that they appear scattered. Refer to the photo on page 39.
2. Sew the blocks together in rows. Press the seams in opposite directions from row to row. Sew the rows together.
3. Measure the quilt top for borders as described in "Adding Borders" on page 24. From the border fabric, cut 2 strips, each 4" wide by the length of your quilt top. Sew the strips to opposite sides of the quilt top. Press the seams toward the border.
4. Cut 2 strips, each 4" wide by the width of your quilt top, including the side borders. Sew the strips to the top and bottom edges of the quilt top. Press the seams toward the border.

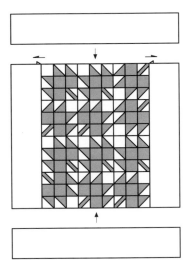

Quilt Finishing

Refer to "Quilt Finishing" on pages 24–25.

1. Layer the quilt top with batting and backing; baste. Quilt as desired, using black quilting thread to emphasize the stitches.

Suggestion

Quilt with an allover fan design. See the template on page 88.

2. Bind the edges of the quilt
3. Tea dye if desired.
4. Press the quilt.

Trick or Treat

Finished Quilt Size: 17¼" x 24½"

Trick or Treat *by Little Quilts, 1994, Marietta, Georgia, 17¼" x 24½".*
Pirates! Gypsies! Ghosts! Treats, not tricks, are in the little packages.

Dutchman's Puzzle
Finished Size: 5"
Templates: FF, Z

Basket
Finished Size: 5"
Templates:
CC, DD, EE, FF

Small Ninepatch
Finished Size: 2¼"
Template: O

House
Finished Size: 5"
Templates:
E, F, G, H, I, J, K, M

Tumbling Block
(Variation)
Finished Size: 5"
Templates: JJ, Y

Materials: 44"-wide fabric

¼ yd. total assorted
blacks for blocks
¼ yd. total assorted greens for blocks
¼ yd. total assorted oranges for blocks
½ yd. total assorted golds for blocks
¼ yd. total assorted browns
¼ yd. for binding
⅝ yd. for backing
20" x 27" piece of thin batting

Block Cutting and Assembly

Rotary-cut the required pieces for each block, or use the appropriate templates if you prefer to hand piece.

Dutchman's Puzzle Blocks

For template cutting, use Templates FF and Z on page 81.

1. From the black and green fabrics, rotary-cut a total of 32 squares, each 1¾" x 1¾", or cut 32 triangles (Template FF).
2. From the orange and gold fabrics, rotary-cut a total of 16 rectangles, each 1¾" x 3", or cut 16 triangles (Template Z).
3. If you rotary-cut the pieces, make 16 flying

geese units, following the shortcut directions on page 27. If you used templates, sew small triangles (piece FF) to each short side of each large triangle (piece Z).

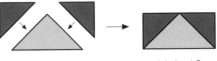

Make 16

4. Sew the completed units together in pairs and press the seam toward the large triangle in each unit.

Make 8

5. Arrange the completed units to make 2 blocks. Sew the units together in rows, pressing the seams in opposite directions from row to row. Sew the rows together to complete each block.

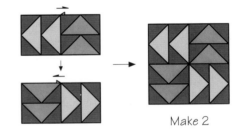

Make 2

Basket Block

For template cutting, use Templates CC, DD, EE, and FF on page 81.

1. From 1 orange, 1 gold, and 1 brown fabric, rotary-cut a 2⅛" square for a total of 3 squares. Cut each square once diagonally for a total of 6 triangles. Or, cut 2 triangles (Template FF) from each of the 3 fabrics.
2. Rotary-cut a 3⅜" square from each of 2 brown fabrics. Cut each square once diagonally for a total of 4 triangles. Set 2 triangles aside. Or, cut 1 triangle (Template EE) from each of 2 brown fabrics.
3. From the background fabric, cut:
   2 squares, each 2⅛" x 2⅛"; cut each square once diagonally for a total of 4 triangles. Or, cut 4 triangles (Template FF).

2 rectangles, each 1¾" x 3", or cut 2 rectangles (Template DD).

1 square, 1¾" x 1¾", or cut 1 square, (Template CC).

1 square, 3⅜" x 3⅜"; cut once diagonally. Set aside 1 of the triangles for another project. Or, cut 1 triangle (Template EE).

4. Arrange the pieces and sew them together, following the directions for "Candy Baskets" on pages 33–34. Make 1 block.

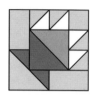

Make 1

Scrappy Ninepatch Block

Use Template O on page 79 to cut squares and assemble 12 blocks as shown below, or follow the directions on page 26 for the "Scrappy Ninepatch Blocks" shortcut.

1. From assorted fabrics, cut 108 squares (Template O).

2. Arrange the squares as desired to make 12 Ninepatch blocks. Sew the squares together in rows, pressing the seams in opposite directions from row to row. Sew the rows together to complete each block.

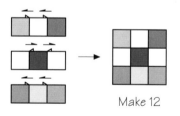

Make 12

House Block

Use Templates E, F, G, H, I, J, K, and M on page 78.

Because of the many inset pieces in this block, we suggest that you hand piece it. No rotary-cutting directions are given.

1. Referring to the chart above right, cut the required pieces from each fabric.

Fabric	No. of Pieces	Template
Gold	2	M
	2	E
	2	F
	1	H
Black	1	E
	1	G
	1	J
	1	J reversed
	1	E
Brown	1	K
Orange	1	I
	2	E

2. Arrange the pieces as shown.

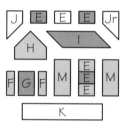

3. Assemble 1 House block as shown on page 56 for "Little Amish Houses."

Tumbling Block (Variation)

Use Templates JJ, KK, and Y on pages 80 and 82.

1. From assorted fabrics of your choice, cut 4 diamonds (Template JJ) and 2 hexagons (Template KK).

2. From a coordinating fabric of your choice, cut 2 pieces, each 4" x 5", for the lining.

3. From black fabric, cut 2 squares (Template Y).

4. Sew 2 diamonds (piece JJ) together and press the seam open. Repeat with the remaining diamonds.

Make 2

5. Place each double-diamond unit face down on the right side of a 4" x 5" fabric square; stitch ¼" from the raw edges of the diamonds. Trim excess lining next to the raw edges and clip across corners.

6. Make a small slit in the lining and turn the unit right-side out through the slit. Press.

Slit lining for turning.

7. Turn under and press ¼" on 2 adjacent edges of each hexagon (piece KK) as shown.

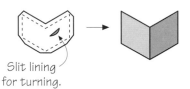

8. Center each hexagon on a black background square (piece Y), placing the folded edges at the top. Appliqué in place along the folded edges. Position a double-diamond unit on top of the hexagon, aligning the outer points of the diamonds with the corners of the hexagon. If necessary, trim the outer edges of the hexagon so they don't extend beyond the diamond unit. Appliqué the outer edges only, leaving the upper edge of the diamond unit unstitched to create a pocket.

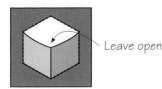

Leave open

Quilt Top Assembly

1. From assorted fabrics, cut 17 sashing strips, each 2¾" x 5½".
2. Referring to the quilt photo on page 42, arrange the quilt blocks, sashing strips, and small Ninepatch blocks in horizontal rows.
3. Sew the blocks and sashing strips together in rows. Press all seams toward the sashing strips.

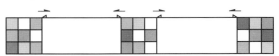

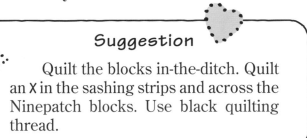

4. Sew rows together, matching all seams.

Quilt Finishing

Refer to "Quilt Finishing" on pages 24–25.
1. Layer the quilt top with batting and backing; baste. Quilt as desired.

Suggestion

Quilt the blocks in-the-ditch. Quilt an X in the sashing strips and across the Ninepatch blocks. Use black quilting thread.

2. Bind the edges of the quilt.
3. Tea dye if desired.
4. Press the quilt.
5. Place candy or small trinkets in the pockets.

Strippy Crib Quilt

Finished size: 37½" x 38½"

Strippy Crib Quilt *by Little Quilts, 1992, Marietta, Georgia, 37½" x 38½".*
Made with new fabrics, this quilt resembles those from the 1800s.

Strippy Four Patch
Finished Size: 3½"
Template: GG

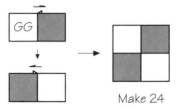

Materials: 44"-wide fabric

½ yd. total assorted
prints for blocks
½ yd. total assorted plaids
and stripes for blocks
1 yd. brown for sashing strips
1 yd. green #1 for border
1¼ yds. green #2 for border
¼ yd. for binding
1¼ yds. for backing
41" x 42" piece of thin batting

Rotary Cutting and Machine Piecing

If you prefer to hand piece, see "Template Cutting and Hand Piecing" at right.

1. Sew 2¼"-wide strips together at random as shown for "Simple Four Patch Blocks" on page 26; crosscut a total of 48 segments, each 2¼"-wide, from the strip units.
2. Sew pairs of segments together to make 24 Four Patch blocks.

Make 24

3. For side setting triangles, cut 10 squares, each 6¼" x 6¼", and cut twice diagonally for a total of 40 side setting triangles. See "Quarter-Square Triangles" on page 26.
4. For corner triangles, cut 8 squares, each 3⅜" x 3⅜"; cut once diagonally for a total of 16 corner triangles. See "Half-Square Triangles" on page 26.
5. To assemble the quilt, see "Quilt Top Assembly" at right.

Template Cutting and Hand Piecing

Use Templates EE, GG, and II on page 81.
1. Cut 96 squares (Template GG)
2. Arrange 4 squares for each block. Sew the squares together in rows. Press the seams in opposite directions. Sew the rows together to complete each block.

Make 24

3. For side setting triangles, cut 40 triangles (Template II).
4. For corner triangles, cut 16 triangles (Template EE).

Quilt Top Assembly

1. Arrange the blocks and triangles to make 4 pieced strips. Sew together in diagonal rows, adding the top and bottom corner triangles last.

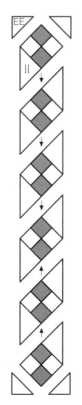

2. From brown fabric, cut 3 sashing strips, each 3½" x 30½".
3. Arrange the pieced strips with brown sashing strips between them. Sew the strips together and press the seams toward the sashing strips.
4. Measure the quilt top for borders as described in "Adding Borders" on page 24. From green #1, cut 2 strips, each 4½" wide by the width of your quilt top. Sew the strips to the top and bottom edges of the quilt top and press the seams toward the border.
5. From green #2, cut 2 strips, each 4½" wide by the length of your quilt top, including the top and bottom borders. Sew the strips to opposite sides of the quilt top. Press the seams toward the borders.

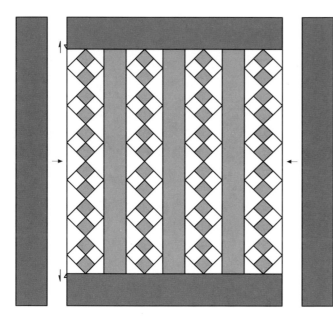

Quilt Finishing

Refer to "Quilt Finishing" on pages 24–25.

1. Layer the quilt top with batting and backing; baste. Quilt as desired.

Suggestion

Quilt an allover design, such as "Fan Quilting," using the pattern on page 88.

2. Bind the edges of the quilt.
3. Tea dye if desired.
4. Press the quilt.

Open Me First!

Finished Quilt Size: 20½" x 20½"

Open Me First! *by Little Quilts, 1994, Marietta, Georgia, 20½" x 20½".*
Good things come in small packages! Choose fabrics for any holiday or occasion. Quilted by Janet Rawls.

Tumbling Block
Finished Size: 2"
Template: JJ

Materials: 44"-wide fabric

⅜ yd. for background squares
⅛ yd. total assorted reds*
for the blocks
⅛ yd. total assorted greens* for the blocks
⅛ yd. total assorted golds* for the blocks
⅔ yd. green plaid for borders
¼ yd. for binding
⅔ yd. for backing
24" x 24" piece of thin batting
2½ yds. ⅜"-wide ribbon
9 assorted buttons

If you wish, use pieces from your basket of 2¼"-wide strips.

Cutting and Sewing

Because of the small pieces and inset seams, we recommend hand-piecing this quilt. No rotary-cutting instructions are given.

Use Templates Y and JJ on pages 80 and 82.

1. From the background fabric, cut 9 squares (Template Y).
2. From the assorted red, green, and gold fabrics, cut 9 diamonds (Template JJ) of each color. You will have a total of 27 diamonds.

2¼"-wide strip

3. Sew a red, green, and gold diamond together as shown. Press the seams toward the darker fabric where possible. Press the seams open if you wish.

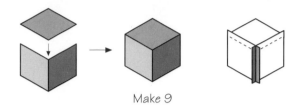

Make 9

4. Press under ¼" on all edges of each Tumbling Block.
5. Fold each background square in half twice and finger-press.
6. To center a Tumbling Block on each background square, push a pin through the center of the tumbling-block unit and insert it through the intersection of the 2 fold lines in the center of the block. Align the top and bottom points of the Tumbling block with the fold lines, keeping the gold fabric at the top. Appliqué in place. Refer to "Hand Appliqué" on page 22.

Quilt Top Assembly

1. Arrange the blocks as desired, referring to the quilt photo on page 49.
2. Sew the blocks together in rows. Press the seams in opposite directions from row to row; then sew the rows together.
3. Measure the quilt top for borders as described in "Adding Borders" on page 24. From the green plaid, cut 2 strips, each 3" wide by the length of your quilt top. Sew the strips to opposite sides of the quilt top. Press the seams toward the borders.

4. Cut 2 strips, each 3" wide by the width of your quilt top, including the side borders. Sew the strips to the top and bottom edges of the quilt top. Press the seams toward the borders.

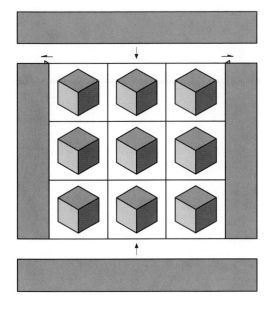

Quilt Finishing

Refer to "Quilt Finishing" on pages 24–25.

1. Layer the quilt top with batting and backing; baste. Quilt as desired.

Refer to "Quilt Finishing" on pages 24–25.

Refer to "Quilt Finishing" on pages 24–25.

Suggestion

Quilt around the appliqué and in the seams. Quilt ¼" inside each background square. Quilt a line 1¼" from the seam inside the border.

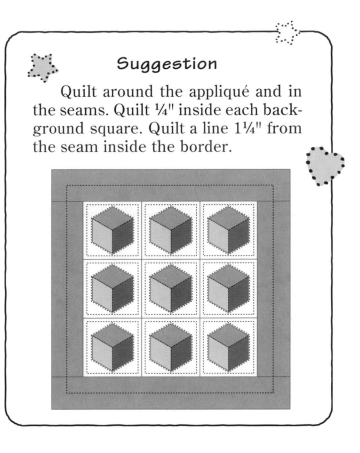

2. Bind the edges of the quilt.
3. Tea dye if desired.
4. Press the quilt.
5. Attach a bow and button to the top of each package. Cut a piece of ribbon approximately 8" to 9" inches long. Without tying the ribbon, fold it to form a bow. Sew a button in the center of the bow.

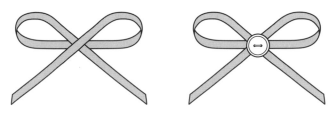

Mr. Snowman Quilt

Finished Quilt Size: 12½" x 17"

Mr. Snowman Quilt *by Little Quilts, 1994, Marietta, Georgia, 12½" x 17".*
Designs for the Little Hooked Rugs can also be used to make simple, quick quilts.

Half-Square Triangle Block
Finished Size: 1½" x 1½"
Template: N

Materials: 44"-wide fabric

9½" x 11" piece of blue
for background
¼ yd. total assorted reds for
triangles, border, and scarf
Assorted scraps of gold
Assorted scraps of green
Small scrap of black for hat
6" x 9" piece of light tan plaid for Snowman
¼ yd. for binding
½ yd. for backing
15" x 20" piece of thin batting
Black embroidery floss
Buttons: 2 medium, 3 tiny black
Fusible web

Cutting

Cut the required pieces using your rotary-cutting equipment, or if you prefer to hand piece, use Template N on page 79 to cut the required number of triangles.

1. From assorted dark fabrics of your choice, cut 12 triangles, or rotary-cut 6 squares, each 2⅜" x 2⅜". Cut the squares once diagonally to yield 12 triangles.
2. From assorted light fabrics of your choice, cut 12 triangles, or rotary-cut 6 squares, each 2⅜" x 2⅜". Cut the squares once diagonally to yield 12 triangles.
3. Sew each dark triangle to a light triangle to make 12 half-square triangle blocks.

Appliqué

Use Template SS on page 79 and the Snowman, Scarf, and Hat templates on page 84.

Refer to "Hand Appliqué" and "Fusible Appliqué" on page 22.

1. Cut 1 snowman and 1 star (Template SS).
2. Appliqué the snowman and the star to the 9½" x 11" piece of background fabric. Refer to the illustration below for proper placement.

Little Tip

If the background fabric shows through the snowman, either line him or carefully cut away the background fabric behind him, leaving a ¼"-wide seam allowance all around.

3. Apply fusible web to the wrong side of small pieces of black and red fabric, following the manufacturer's directions. Place the hat and scarf templates right side down on the paper backing. Trace around them and cut them out. Fuse the pieces in place. Buttonhole-stitch around the edges of the star, hat, and scarf (page 23).
4. Chain-stitch the arms, using six strands of black embroidery floss.

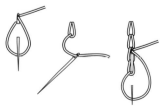

Chain Stitch

Quilt Top Assembly

1. Join 6 half-square triangle blocks to form a row. Make 2 rows.

Make 2

2. Sew a row to the top and bottom edges of the Snowman block. Press the seams toward the Snowman block.
3. From the assorted red fabrics, cut 2¼"-wide strips in random lengths.
4. Sew these strips together to make a strip approximately 60" long.

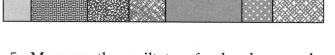

5. Measure the quilt top for borders as described in "Adding Borders" on page 24. From the pieced strip, cut 2 pieces, each the length of your quilt top. Sew the strips to opposite sides of the quilt top. Press the seams toward the borders.
6. From the pieced strip, cut 2 pieces, each the width of your quilt top, including the side borders. Sew the strips to the top and bottom edges of the quilt top. Press the seams toward the borders.

Quilt Finishing

Refer to "Quilt Finishing" on pages 24–25.
1. Layer quilt top with batting and backing; baste. Quilt as desired.

Suggestion

Quilt around the appliqué. Quilt random swirling lines on the background. Quilt the triangle border in-the-ditch. Quilt a single line through the center of the border, ¾" from the seam.

2. Bind the edges of the quilt.
3. Tea dye if desired.
4. Press the quilt.
5. Sew buttons on the snowman, referring to the quilt photo on page 52 for placement.

CELEBRATING HOMELAND

Houses, trees, and flags remind us of our own special place on the earth, our homeland.

Little Amish Houses

Finished Quilt Size: 18½" x 24½"

Little Amish Houses *by Little Quilts, 1994, Marietta, Georgia, 18½" x 24½".*
An Amish neighborhood of simple, tidy houses. Which house would you like to live in?
Quilted by Janet Rawls.

House
Finished Size: 5"
Templates: E, F, G, H, I, J, K, M

Materials: 44"-wide fabric

⅛ yd. total assorted red
solids for houses
⅛ yd. total assorted blue solids for houses
⅛ yd. total assorted green solids for houses
⅛ yd. total assorted brown solids for houses
⅛ yd. total assorted gold solids for houses
⅛ yd. total assorted purple
solids for corner squares
¼ yd. purple solid for sashing strips
¾ yd. black solid for background and borders
¼ yd. for binding
⅝ yd. for backing
21" x 27" piece of thin batting

Cutting and Sewing

Because of the many inset pieces, we suggest that you hand-piece this quilt. No rotary-cutting instructions are given.

Use Templates E, F, G, H, I, J, K, L, and M on page 78.

1. From the assorted fabrics for houses, cut:
   6 Template I (roofs);
   12 Template E (chimneys);
   6 Template E, 6 Template J, and 6 Template J reversed (sky);
   6 Template G (doors);
   12 Template F (house fronts);
   6 Template H (front upper story);
   6 Template E (windows);
   12 Template E and 12 Template M (sides of the houses);
   6 Template K (grass).

2. Arrange the pieces as shown.

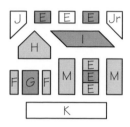

3. Sew pieces into units as shown; then sew the units together to make 6 House blocks.

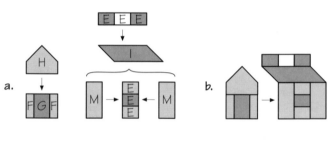

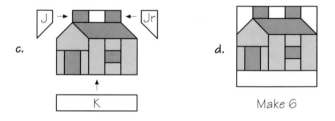

Make 6

Quilt Top Assembly

1. From the purple solid for sashing, cut 17 strips (Template K).
2. From the assorted purple fabrics, cut 12 corner squares (Template L).

3. Arrange the houses, sashing strips, and corner squares in rows.

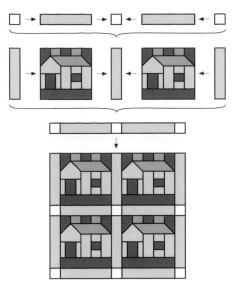

4. Sew blocks and sashing strips together in rows. Press seams toward sashing strips.
5. Measure the quilt top for borders as described in "Adding Borders" on page 24. From the black solid, cut 2 strips, each 3" wide by the length of your quilt top. Sew the strips to opposite sides of the quilt top. Press the seams toward the borders.

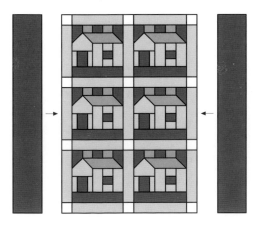

6. From the black solid, cut 2 strips, each 3" wide by the width of your quilt top, including the side borders. Sew the strips to the top

and bottom edges of the quilt top. Press the seams toward the borders.

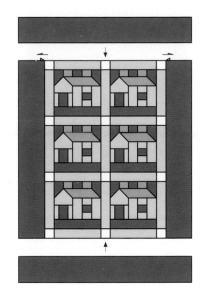

Quilt Finishing

Refer to "Quilt Finishing" on pages 24–25.
1. Layer the quilt top with batting and backing; baste. Quilt as desired.

Suggestion

Quilt houses in-the-ditch. Quilt an X in the corner squares. Quilt a cable design in the border, using the pattern on page 88. Use the corner pattern to join cables. If needed, extend lines to make cables fit. Use black quilting thread.

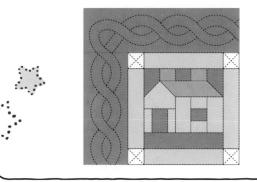

2. Bind the edges of the quilt.
3. Tea dye if desired.
4. Press the quilt.

Pine Trees

Finished Quilt Size: 21" x 28"

Pine Trees *by Little Quilts, 1994, Marietta, Georgia, 21" x 28".*
Standing so tall they seem to touch the sky, these Georgia pines can grow anywhere.
Quilted by Janet Rawls.

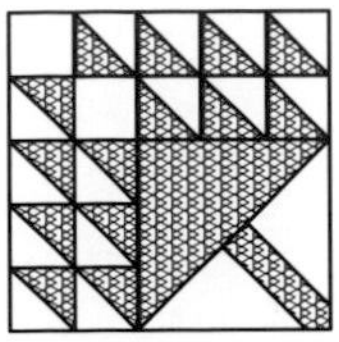

Pine Tree
Finished Size: 5"
Templates: L, U, B

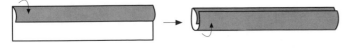

Materials: 44"-wide fabric

½ yd. total assorted tans
¼ yd. total assorted greens
¾ yd. gold for inner border
¾ yd. red for outer border
¼ yd. for binding
¾ yd. for backing
23" x 30" piece of thin batting

Rotary Cutting and Machine Piecing

If you prefer to hand piece, see "Template Cutting" below right.

1. From the tan fabrics, cut:
   2 squares, each 5½" x 5½", for the alternate blocks.
   2 squares, each 8¼" x 8¼"; cut twice diagonally for 8 side setting triangles. You will have 2 extra triangles. Set them aside for another project.
   2 squares, each 4⅜" x 4⅜"; cut once diagonally for 4 corner triangles.
   42 squares, each 1⅞" x 1⅞"; cut once diagonally for 84 triangles.
   12 tan squares, each 1½" x 1½".
   3 squares, each 3⅞" x 3⅞"; cut once diagonally for 6 triangles for the trunk background.
2. From the assorted green fabrics, cut:
   42 squares, each 1⅞" x 1⅞"; cut once diagonally for 84 triangles.
   3 squares, each 3⅞" x 3⅞"; cut once diagonally for 6 triangles.
3. For the tree trunks, cut 6 bias strips from green fabric, each 1¼" x 3". Fold the strips into thirds and press.

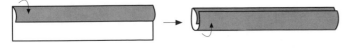

4. Appliqué 1 strip on each large tan triangle as shown, using matching thread. Trim excess fabric at the point.
5. Sew each green triangle to a tan triangle. Press the seams toward the darker color. 
6. Arrange the pieces for each of the blocks and sew together as shown.

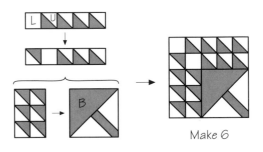

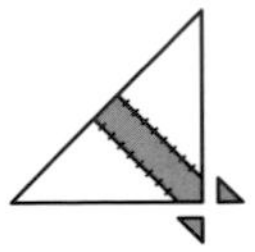

Make 6

7. To assemble the quilt top, see "Quilt Top Assembly" on page 60.

Template Cutting

Use Templates B, L, U, W, X, and Y on page 80.

1. From the assorted tan fabrics, cut:
   2 squares (Template Y);
   6 triangles (Template W) for side setting triangles;
   4 triangles (Template X) for corner triangles;
   84 triangles (Template U);
   12 squares (Template L);
   6 assorted tan triangles (Template B).
2. From the assorted green fabrics, cut:
   84 triangles (Template U);
   6 triangles (Template B).
3. For tree trunks, cut 6 bias strips from green fabric, each 1" x 3". Make stems and appliqué each to a large tan triangle as shown for step 3 of "Rotary Cutting and Machine Piecing" at left.
4. Assemble the block as shown in "Rotary Cutting and Machine Piecing" at left.

Quilt Top Assembly

1. Arrange the blocks, side setting triangles, and corner triangles in diagonal rows as shown. Sew the blocks together in rows; press the seams in opposite directions from row to row.
2. Sew the rows together, matching the seams carefully.
3. Add the corner triangles last.

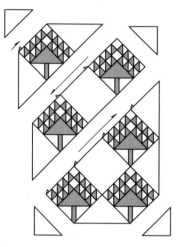

4. Measure the quilt top for borders as described in "Adding Borders" on page 24. From the gold fabric, cut 2 strips, each 1¼" wide by the length of your quilt top. Sew the strips to opposite sides of the quilt top. Press the seams and all remaining border seams toward the borders.
5. From the gold fabric, cut 2 strips, each 1¼" wide by the width of your quilt top, including the side borders. Sew the strips to the top and bottom edges of the quilt top.
6. From the red fabric, cut 2 strips, each 3" wide by the length of your quilt top. Sew the strips to opposite sides of the quilt top.
7. From the red fabric, cut 2 pieces, each 3" wide by the width of your quilt top, including the side borders. Sew the strips to the top and bottom edges of the quilt top.

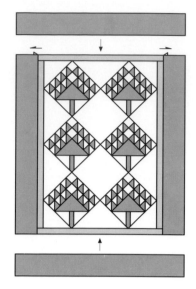

Quilt Finishing

Refer to "Quilt Finishing" on pages 24–25.
1. Layer the quilt top with batting and backing; baste. Quilt as desired.

Suggestion

Quilt the Tree blocks and the inner border in-the-ditch. Quilt stars (Template SS on page 79) in the tan squares, setting triangles, and outer border; quilt a moon in the upper corner. Connect the stars with a wavy line.

2. Bind the edges of the quilt.
3. Tea dye if desired.
4. Press the quilt.

Going South for Winter

Finished Quilt Size: 17" x 21¾"

Going South for Winter *by Little Quilts, 1994, Marietta, Georgia, 17" x 21¾".*
Flying overhead in perfect formation, these geese are headed for warmer weather.
Quilted by Janet Rawls.

Flying Geese
Finished Size: 1¼" x 2½"
Templates: FF, Z

Materials: 44"-wide fabric

Use small amounts of assorted
fall colors and "magic" fabrics to
make the flying geese.
Assorted 1¾"-wide dark strips for flying geese
Assorted 1¾"-wide light strips for background
½ yd. green for sashing strips
½ yd. blue for inner border
Assorted strips, each 2½" wide, in varying
lengths for border
¼ yd. for binding
⅝ yd. for backing
21" x 26" piece of thin batting

Rotary Cutting and Machine Piecing

Use 1¾"-wide strips from your basket of
reserved strips to cut pieces. If you prefer to
hand piece, see "Template Cutting and Hand
Piecing" below.
1. From the assorted dark strips, cut a total of
   39 rectangles, each 1¾" x 3".
2. From the assorted light strips, cut a total of
   78 squares, each 1¾" x 1¾".
3. Make 39 blocks, following the directions for
   "Flying Geese" on page 27.
4. To complete the quilt, see "Quilt Top Assembly" above right.

Template Cutting and Hand Piecing

Use Templates FF and Z on page 81.
1. From the assorted dark strips, cut a total of
   39 triangles (Template Z).
2. From the assorted light strips, cut a total of
   78 triangles (Template FF).
3. Sew a light triangle to each side of each dark
   triangle.

Make 39

Quilt Top Assembly

Note

When sewing Flying Geese blocks
together, place the blocks with right
sides together and stitch with the point
of the large triangle on top. Sew a
"thread's width" away from the point of
the triangle where the seams cross.

1. Sew 13 Flying Geese blocks together to
   make a row.
2. From green fabric, cut 2 sashing strips,
   each 2½" x 16¾".
3. Sew flying geese rows to sashing strips as
   shown. Align the blocks across the quilt.
   Press the seams toward the sashing strips.

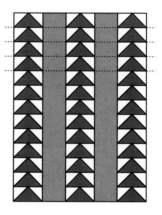

4. Measure the quilt top for borders as described in "Adding Borders" on page 24.
   From the blue fabric, cut 2 strips, each 1"
   wide by the length of your quilt top. Sew
   the strips to opposite sides of the quilt top.
   Press the seams and all remaining border
   seams toward the inner border.

5. From the blue fabric, cut 2 strips, each 1" wide by the width of your quilt top, including the side borders. Sew the strips to the top and bottom edges of the quilt.

6. For the pieced outer border, join the assorted 2½"-wide strips end to end to create one continuous strip, approximately 75" long.

7. From the pieced strip, cut 2 strips, each the length of your quilt. Sew the strips to the sides of the quilt top.

8. From the pieced strip, cut 2 strips, each the width of your quilt top, including the side borders. Sew the strips to the top and bottom edges of the quilt top.

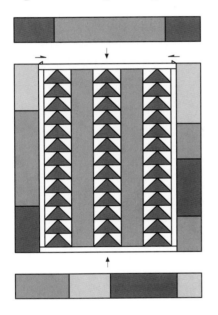

Quilt Finishing

Refer to "Quilt Finishing" on pages 24–25.
1. Layer the quilt top with batting and backing; baste. Quilt as desired.

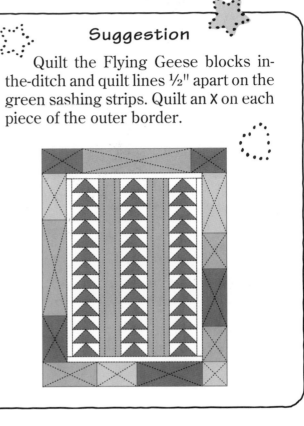

Suggestion

Quilt the Flying Geese blocks in-the-ditch and quilt lines ½" apart on the green sashing strips. Quilt an X on each piece of the outer border.

2. Bind the edges of the quilt.
3. Tea dye if desired.
4. Press the quilt.

America

Finished Quilt Size: 35½" x 35½"

America *by Little Quilts, 1994, Marietta, Georgia, 35½" x 35½".*
Everyone comes together in celebration! Personalize this quilt to represent your country.

Alphabet Block
Finished Size: 5"
Templates: Y, Letters

Basket
Finished Size: 5"
Templates: CC, DD, EE, FF

Pine Tree
Finished Size: 5"
Templates: L, U, B

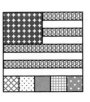

Flag
Finished Size: 5"
Templates: L, NN, OO, PP

House
Finished Size: 5"
Templates: E, F, G, H, I, J, K, M

Dutchman's Puzzle
Finished Size: 5"
Templates: FF, Z

Flying Geese
Finished Size:
1¼" x 2½"
Templates: FF, Z

Star
Finished Size: 5"
Templates: Y, TT

Heart
Finished Size: 5"
Templates: Y, QQ

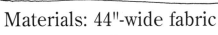

Materials: 44"-wide fabric

1½ yds. total assorted dark
and light fabrics, including red, tan,
and blue, for blocks and appliqué
⅞ yd. red for inner border
1 yd. blue for middle border
⅜ yd. total assorted red prints for
sawtooth border
⅜ yd. total assorted gold prints for
sawtooth border
¼ yd. for binding
1¼ yds. for backing
40" x 40" piece of thin batting
Embroidery floss: red, gold, and blue
Assorted buttons
Fusible web

Rotary Cutting

If you prefer to hand piece, see "Template Cutting" on page 66.

FLAG BLOCKS

1. To make 5 Flag blocks, cut several 1"-wide strips from the assorted red and tan fabrics for blocks.
2. From the 1"-wide red strips, cut 10 rectangles, each 1" x 3", and 10 rectangles, each 1" x 5½".
3. From the 1"-wide tan strips, cut 10 rectangles, each 1" x 3", and 10 rectangles, each 1" x 5½".
4. From the blue fabric, cut 5 rectangles, each 2½" x 3".
5. From the assorted fabrics for blocks, cut 25 squares, each 1½" x 1½".
6. Arrange the units and sew them together as shown.

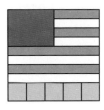

Make 5

FLYING GEESE BLOCKS

1. From the assorted gold fabrics, cut 52 rectangles, each 1¾" x 3", and 4 squares, each 1¾" x 1¾". Reserve the squares for outerborder corners.
2. From the assorted red fabrics, cut 104 squares, each 1¾" x 1¾".
3. Make 52 blocks, referring to "Flying Geese" on page 27, and reserve for the sawtooth border.

Make 52

4. To construct the remaining blocks and complete the quilt, see "More Cutting, More Blocks" at right.

Template Cutting

FLAG BLOCKS

Use Templates NN, OO, PP, and L on pages 78 and 82.

1. From the assorted red fabrics for blocks, cut 10 rectangles (Template OO) and 10 rectangles (Template PP).
2. From the assorted tan fabrics for blocks, cut 10 rectangles (Template OO) and 10 rectangles (Template PP).
3. From the assorted blue fabrics for blocks, cut 5 rectangles (Template NN).
4. From the assorted fabrics for blocks, cut 25 squares (Template L).
5. Arrange units and sew together as shown.

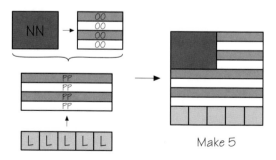

Make 5

FLYING GEESE BLOCKS

Use Templates CC, FF, and Z on page 81.

1. From the assorted gold fabrics, cut 52 triangles (Template Z). Cut 4 squares (Template CC) and reserve them for the outerborder corners.
2. From the assorted red fabrics, cut 104 triangles (Template FF).
3. Make 52 Flying Geese blocks, referring to step 3 of "Template Cutting and Hand Piecing" on page 62. Reserve for the sawtooth border.

More Cutting, More Blocks

1. Cut the pieces for and make:
   2 Dutchman's Puzzle blocks. See "Trick or Treat" on pages 42–45.
   2 Tree blocks. See "Pine Trees" on pages 58–60.
   3 Basket blocks. See "Candy Baskets" on pages 32–34.
2. From the assorted light fabrics, cut 11 squares, each 5½" x 5½", for the Alphabet blocks, or use Template Y.

Appliqué Blocks

Refer to "Alphabet Appliqué" and "Buttonhole Stitch" on page 23. Use the appropriate letter templates and Templates QQ and TT on pages 79–80 and 86–87.

1. Cut the appropriate letters from blue fabric. Appliqué them to the reserved squares of background fabric. Buttonhole stitch around the edges with red embroidery floss.
2. From the assorted dark and light fabrics, cut 2 hearts (Template QQ) and 2 stars (Template TT). Appliqué them to the background squares. Buttonhole stitch around the edges with red, gold, and blue embroidery floss.

Quilt Top Assembly

1. Arrange the blocks as illustrated.
2. Sew blocks together in rows. Press the seams in opposite directions from row to row.
3. Join the rows, matching seams.
4. From the red fabric for the inner border, cut 2 strips, each 1½" x 25½". Sew the strips to opposite sides of the quilt top. Press the seams and all remaining inner and middle border seams toward the border.
5. From the red fabric for the inner border, cut 2 strips, each 1½" x 27½". Sew the strips to the top and bottom edges of the quilt top.
6. From the blue fabric, cut 2 strips, each 3¼" x 27½". Sew the strips to opposite sides of the quilt top.
7. From the blue fabric, cut 2 strips, each 3¼" x 33". Sew the strips to the top and bottom edges of the quilt top.

Sawtooth Border

1. Sew 13 Flying Geese blocks together, side by side, to form border strips. Make 4 strips.

2. Sew a strip of flying geese to 2 opposite sides of the quilt.
3. Sew a reserved gold square to each end of the 2 remaining flying geese strips. Press the seams toward the gold squares.
4. Sew the strips to the top and bottom edges of the quilt top. Press the seams toward the blue border.

Quilt Finishing

Refer to "Quilt Finishing" on pages 24–25.

1. Layer the quilt top with batting and backing; baste. Quilt as desired.

Suggestion

Quilt pieced blocks in-the-ditch; quilt ¼" inside the edges of the appliqué blocks. Quilt a wavy line across the flag stripes. Quilt stars (Template SS on page 79) in the border and connect them with a wavy line.

2. Bind the edges of the quilt.
3. Tea dye if desired.
4. Press the quilt.
5. Sew buttons on the Flag blocks. See the photo on page 64 for placement ideas.

Children are one of the best reasons to celebrate. We mark passages
in their lives, such as birth, graduation, college, and marriage.
A Little Quilt is the perfect gift for any of these occasions.

Ninepatch Doll Quilt

Finished Quilt Size: 15½" x 18⅝"

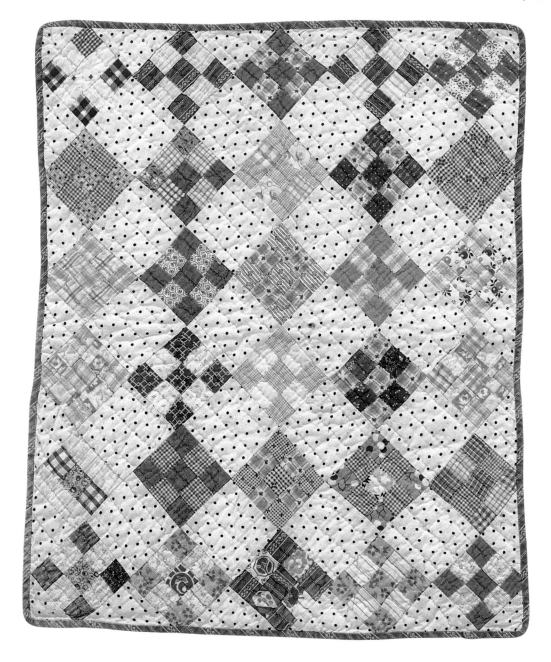

Antique Ninepatch Doll Quilt, *1930s, 15½" x 18⅝". Sweet little Ninepatch blocks combine
with polka dots for a cheerful doll quilt. Collection of Mary Ellen Von Holt.*

Some blocks in the antique quilt pictured were made with only two fabrics, while others were made with several "look alike" fabrics.

Small Ninepatch
Finished Size: 2¼"
Template: O

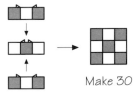

Materials: 44"-wide fabric

⅓ yd. total assorted fabric scraps
or assorted 1¼"-wide strips
⅓ yd. polka dot fabric for setting
squares and triangles
¼ yd. for binding
½ yd. for backing
18" x 21" piece of thin batting

Rotary Cutting and Machine Piecing

If you prefer to hand piece, see "Template Cutting and Hand Piecing" below.

1. Choose dark and light strips from your basket of 1¼"-wide strips, or cut 1¼"-wide strips from scraps. Make strip units as described for the "Scrappy Ninepatch Block" shortcut on page 26.
2. Cut a total of 60 segments with the light fabric in the center and 30 segments with the dark fabric in the center.
3. Make 30 Ninepatch blocks.
4. From the polka dot fabric, cut:
   20 squares, each 2¾" x 2¾", for setting squares.
   5 squares, each 4½" x 4½", for side setting triangles. Cut twice diagonally for 20 triangles (there will be 2 extra).
   2 squares, each 2⅜" x 2⅜", for corner triangles. Cut once diagonally for 4 triangles.
5. To complete the quilt top, see "Quilt Top Assembly" at right.

Template Cutting and Hand Piecing

Use Templates O, P, Q, and V on page 79.
1. From the assorted fabric scraps, cut 150 dark squares and 120 light squares

(Template O). Arrange and sew the squares together in rows as shown. Press seams toward dark fabric.

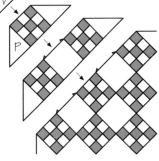

Make 30

2. From the polka dot fabric, cut:
   20 squares (Template Q), for setting squares;
   18 triangles (Template P), for side setting triangles;
   4 triangles (Template V), for corner triangles.

Quilt Top Assembly

1. Arrange blocks, side, and corner triangles in diagonal rows.
2. Sew blocks and triangles together in rows. Press seams toward the setting squares.
3. Sew the rows together. Add the corner triangles last.

Quilt Finishing

Refer to "Quilt Finishing" on pages 24–25.
1. Layer the quilt top with batting and backing; baste. Quilt as desired.

Suggestion

Quilt diagonal lines across the quilt, spacing them approximately ¾" apart.

2. Bind the edges of the quilt.
3. Tea dye if desired.
4. Press the quilt.

Sawtooth Doll Quilt

Finished Size: 10" x 14½"

Antique Sawtooth Doll Quilt, early 1900s, 10" x 14½". Folk art for dolls!
Collection of Mary Ellen Von Holt.

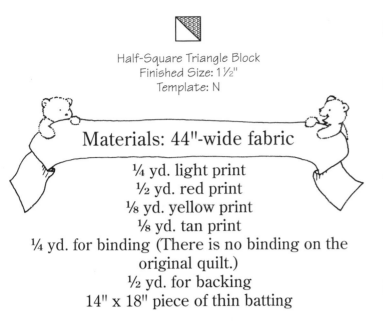

Half-Square Triangle Block
Finished Size: 1½"
Template: N

Materials: 44"-wide fabric

¼ yd. light print
½ yd. red print
⅛ yd. yellow print
⅛ yd. tan print
¼ yd. for binding (There is no binding on the original quilt.)
½ yd. for backing
14" x 18" piece of thin batting

Cutting

Rotary-cut the following pieces, or if you prefer to hand piece, use Template N on page 79 to cut the triangles.

1. From the light print, cut 40 triangles. Or cut 20 squares, each 2⅜" x 2⅜"; cut the squares once diagonally for 40 half-square triangles.
2. From the red print, cut 16 triangles. Or cut 8 squares, each 2⅜" x 2⅜"; cut the squares once diagonally for 16 half-square triangles.
3. From the yellow print, cut 16 triangles. Or cut 8 squares, each 2⅜" x 2⅜"; cut the squares once diagonally for 16 triangles.
4. From the tan print, cut 8 triangles. Or cut 4 squares, each 2⅜" x 2⅜"; cut the squares once diagonally for 8 half-square triangles.

Quilt Top Assembly

1. Sew each light triangle to a colored triangle to make half-square triangle blocks.

Red
Make 16

Yellow
Make 16

Tan
Make 8

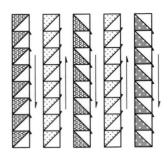

2. Arrange the blocks in rows as shown and sew together.
3. Press seams in opposite directions from row to row. Join the rows, matching the seams.
4. Measure the quilt top for borders as described in "Adding Borders" on page 24. Cut 2 strips from the red print, each 1½" wide by the length of your quilt. Sew the strips to opposite sides of the quilt top and press the seams toward the borders.
5. From the red print, cut 2 strips, each 1½" wide by the width of your quilt, including the side borders. Sew the strips to the top and bottom edges of the quilt top and press.

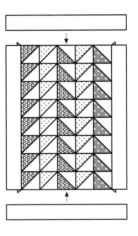

Quilt Finishing

Refer to "Quilt Finishing" on pages 24–25.

1. Layer the quilt top with batting and backing; baste. Quilt as desired.

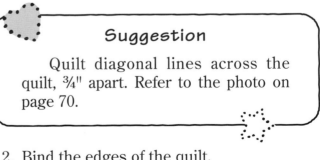

Suggestion

Quilt diagonal lines across the quilt, ¾" apart. Refer to the photo on page 70.

2. Bind the edges of the quilt.
3. Tea dye if desired.
4. Press the quilt.

Alphabet Crib Quilt

Finished Quilt Size: 32½" x 37½"

Alphabet Crib Quilt *by Little Quilts, 1994, Marietta, Georgia. 32½" x 37½". This quilt is easy to make and fun to look at with its many cheerful fabrics. Quilted by Janet Rawls.*

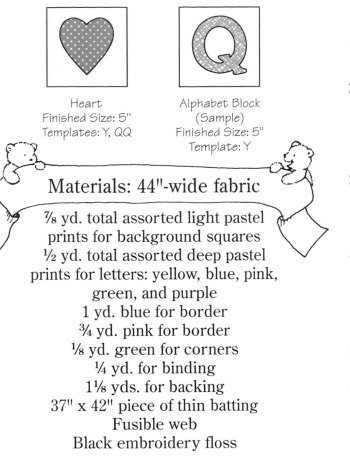

Heart
Finished Size: 5"
Templates: Y, QQ

Alphabet Block
(Sample)
Finished Size: 5"
Template: Y

Materials: 44"-wide fabric

⅞ yd. total assorted light pastel
prints for background squares
½ yd. total assorted deep pastel
prints for letters: yellow, blue, pink,
green, and purple
1 yd. blue for border
¾ yd. pink for border
⅛ yd. green for corners
¼ yd. for binding
1⅛ yds. for backing
37" x 42" piece of thin batting
Fusible web
Black embroidery floss

Block Cutting and Appliqué

1. From assorted light prints, cut 30 squares, each 5½" x 5½", or use Template Y on page 80 to cut 30 squares.
2. From the assorted deep pastel fabrics, cut one of each letter using the templates on pages 86–87.
3. Cut 4 hearts from deep pastel fabrics (Template QQ on page 80).
4. Referring to "Alphabet Appliqué" on page 23, appliqué letters and hearts to the background squares. Buttonhole-stitch around each piece with black thread; refer to "Buttonhole Stitch" on page 23.

Quilt Top Assembly

1. Referring to the quilt photo on page 72, arrange the Heart and Alphabet blocks.
2. Sew blocks together in rows. Press seams in opposite directions from row to row. Sew the rows together.
3. Measure the quilt top through the center as described on page 24. Measure for side *and* top and bottom borders now.
4. From blue fabric, cut 2 strips, each 4" wide by the length of the quilt top. From the pink fabric, cut 2 strips, each 4" wide by the width of the quilt top. From green fabric, cut 4 corner squares, each 4" x 4".
5. Sew the blue strips to opposite sides of the quilt top. Press seams toward the borders.
6. Sew a green square to each end of each pink border strip. Press seams toward borders.

Make 2

7. Sew the pink borders to the top and bottom edges of the quilt. Press the seams toward the borders.

Quilt Finishing

Refer to "Quilt Finishing" on pages 24–25.
1. Layer the quilt top with batting and backing; baste. Quilt as desired.

Suggestion

Quilt around each letter and heart. Quilt ¼" from the seam inside each background square. Crosshatch the border with rows spaced 1¾" apart.

2. Bind the edges of the quilt.
3. Tea dye if desired.
4. Press the quilt.

Rug Hooking

We volunteer each year for a festival in our area that benefits a historic home. We demonstrate quiltmaking, and other craftspeople demonstrate their skills at woodcarving and at making baskets, lace, and dolls. We saw and admired the rug hooking there, and eventually took lessons, attended a "Rug Camp," and made lots of rugs. You might say we were "hooked." These primitive rugs make a nice addition to a home full of quilts.

We make our rugs with narrow strips of 100% wool fabric. Primitive rug hooking requires ¼"-wide strips as opposed to the narrower strips used for traditional rug hooking.

Basic directions are included here. For more information on rug hooking, check your area for classes, or ask your local bookstore or library for books on the subject.

Little Lesson

Primitive rug hooking is not difficult. As a beginner, try to develop a feel for the process. Practice hooking in straight rows and pulling loops to an even height.

SUPPLIES FOR LITTLE RUGS

★ *100% wool fabric.* (You can use 11 to 13 oz. new wool, or old clothing.) Plaids, tweeds, and herringbone styles create interesting designs. Prewash wool in a washing machine with warm

Little hooked rugs and the ingredients needed to make them. Rugs designed by Little Quilts, 1994, Marietta, Georgia. Country House and Bird, *12" x 18"*; Mr. Snowman, *11" x 13½"; and* Hearts and Stars, *12" x 18". Hooked by Lita McCormick, Atlanta, Georgia.*

water and a small amount of laundry detergent, using the gentle cycle. Dry in the dryer using medium heat. This process "felts" the wool.

★ *Primitive rug hook* (looks like a crochet hook with a wood handle).
★ *Primitive burlap or linen* (a good quality in an even weave, available from suppliers).
★ *Rug hooking frame* (you can substitute a quilting hoop).
★ *Scissors or strip-cutting machine.* (You can cut strips by hand, or use a cutter that cuts several strips of an even width at a time. We have heard of people who use sergers without thread and even paper shredders!) Cut strips on the lengthwise grain whenever possible.
★ *Twill rug-binding tape*, 1¼"-wide (or substitute 1¼"-wide strips of wool).
★ *Black permanent-ink pen.*

HOOKING LITTLE RUGS

1. Collect and prewash the wool. You can dye wool using commercial dyes, or use it "as is" in the true primitive way. (Rug hooking books have more information on custom dyeing wool.) You need approximately four to five times the area to be hooked. For example, an area that is 4" x 4" would require a piece of fabric that is 4" x 20". To check the required yardage, you can fold the wool so that it is four or five layers thick and place it on top of the design area to be covered. If the folded wool covers the area to be hooked, you most likely have enough to hook that area.

2. Cut a piece of primitive burlap at least 6" larger than the design all around. Finish the edges with a zigzag stitch or cover them with masking tape to prevent fraying.

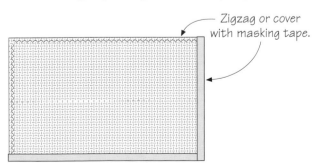

Zigzag or cover with masking tape.

3. Select a design and trace the pattern shapes onto plastic template material. On the burlap, draw around the patterns with the permanent-ink pen.

4. To hook, push the hook from the top through a space in the burlap. Catch a strip of wool underneath and pull it through the burlap to the top to form a loop.

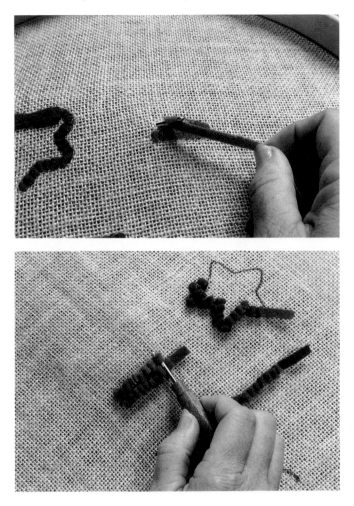

5. Bring all strip ends to the top. Begin a new strip in the space where you finished the previous one. Bring the end of the strip to the top and continue hooking as before.

6. Do not pull a loop through every hole in the burlap. Skip every other hole to avoid packing the loops too tightly. When in doubt, leave one out! The thickness of the wool also determines the spacing.

7. Begin by outlining shapes, staying just inside the drawn line; then fill in the design. Hook the border. Hook the background area last.

8. Trim the ends even with the loops. Loops should be approximately ¼" high.

Little Lesson

To correct loops that are twisted when pulled up, pull the loop higher and straighten the strip with the hook. Then pull the strip back down to the proper height.

9. When the hooking is completed, steam the rug well with a damp cloth and an iron. Press both sides. Allow to dry overnight.

FINISHING LITTLE RUGS

1. Mark a line on the excess burlap 1" from the edge of the design.
2. Sew two rows of zigzag stitches next to each other along this line. Cut away excess burlap beyond this stitching.
3. Draw a diagonal line across the corner and trim away excess burlap, cutting on the line.
4. Place a strip of 1¼"-wide prewashed twill rug binding (or a 1¼"-wide strip of wool) on the top of the rug with the raw edge extending ¼" beyond the hooked edge.

5. Hand stitch close to the hooked edge using heavy thread. Ease binding around corners and overlap the ends where they meet.

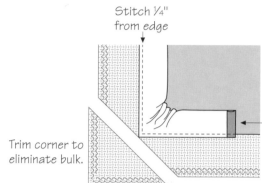

Stitch ¼" from edge

Trim corner to eliminate bulk.

Begin sewing tape here with end folded back.

6. Fold the burlap and binding to the back, miter the corners, and hand stitch to the back of the rug.

Note

You can sew the binding on before hooking the rug. Stitch the binding just outside the line marking the border. Draw a line ¼" from the stitching line to help you place the binding properly. Sew by hand or machine. Hook right up to the edge of the tape. Finish the binding as described above.

LITTLE RUG PROJECTS

1. Assemble your supplies.
2. Make plastic templates of the chosen designs (pages 83–85).
3. With a permanent-ink pen, draw a rectangle of the desired rug size on burlap. The lines should follow the weave of the burlap. If you want to enlarge one of our rug patterns, add more background between the designs and the border. The sizes used in our examples are as follows:

Country House and Bird: 12" x 18"

Mr. Snowman: 11" x 13½"

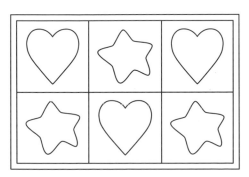

Hearts and Stars: 12" x 18"

4. Draw around the pattern templates on the burlap. (You may want to practice on a piece of paper first; however, the hooking will cover any drawing mistakes.) Center the hearts and stars in 5" squares. Draw lines for borders. Our borders are approximately ½" to 1" all around (2 to 4 rows of hooking).
5. Hook the designs. Remember to include your initials and the year somewhere!
6. Bind the rug (page 76).
7. Press well with a damp cloth. Let dry.
8. Find a place to display your Little Rug.

Rug Hooking Supplies

Joan Moshimer's Rug Hooker Studio
21 North Street, PO Box 351
Kennebunkport, ME 04046-0351
1-800-626-7847

The Dorr Mill Store
PO Box 88
Guild, NH 03754
(603) 863-1197
1-800-846-DORR

Braid-Aid
466 Washington Street
Pembroke, MA 02359
(617) 826-2560

Hooked on Rugs
44492 Midway Drive
Novi, MI 48375
(313) 344-4367

For catalog and mail-order information, send $2.00 to:

Little Quilts
4939 Lower Roswell Rd., Suite 204C
Marietta, GA 30068

Little Quilts fabric is available at your local fabric shop.

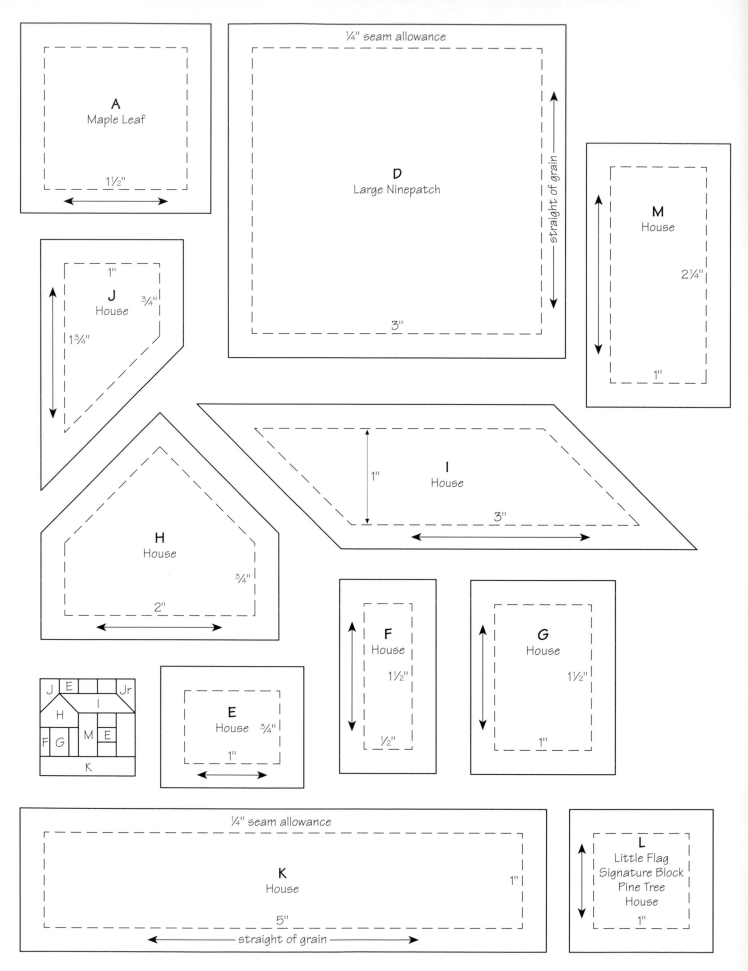

A
Maple Leaf

1½"

¼" seam allowance

D
Large Ninepatch

straight of grain

3"

M
House

2¼"

1"

1"

J
House

¾"

1¾"

I
House

1"

3"

H
House

¾"

2"

F
House

1½"

½"

G
House

1½"

1"

J E Jr
H I
F G M E
K

E
House ¾"

1"

¼" seam allowance

K
House

1"

5"

straight of grain

L
Little Flag
Signature Block
Pine Tree
House

1"

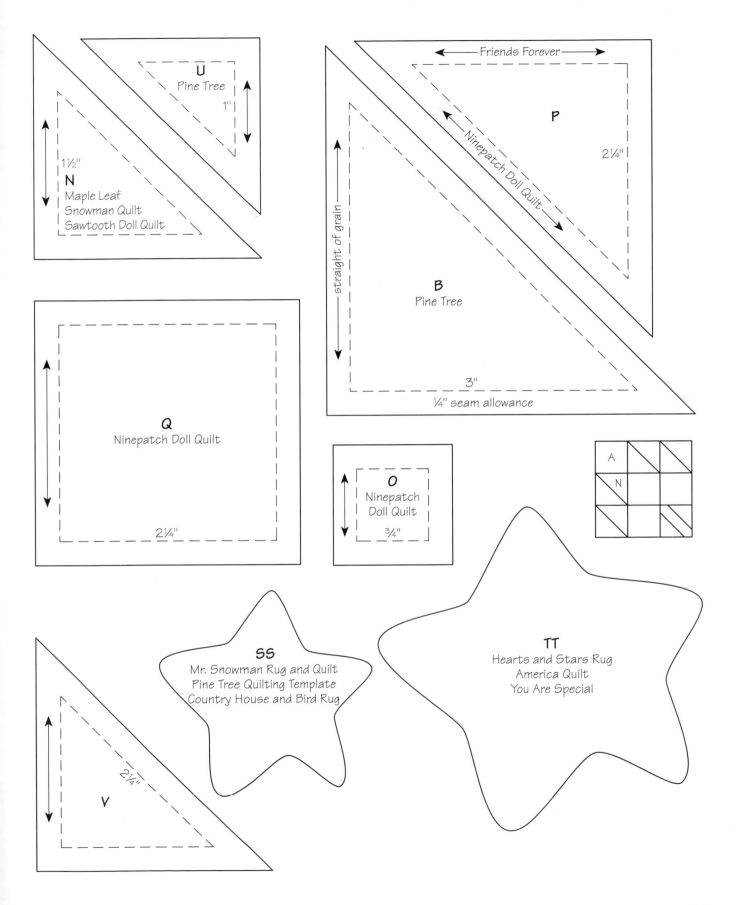

U
Pine Tree
1"

N
Maple Leaf
Snowman Quilt
Sawtooth Doll Quilt
1½"

Friends Forever

P
2¼"

Ninepatch Doll Quilt

straight of grain

B
Pine Tree

3"
¼" seam allowance

Q
Ninepatch Doll Quilt
2¼"

O
Ninepatch
Doll Quilt
¾"

A
N

V
2¼"

SS
Mr. Snowman Rug and Quilt
Pine Tree Quilting Template
Country House and Bird Rug

TT
Hearts and Stars Rug
America Quilt
You Are Special

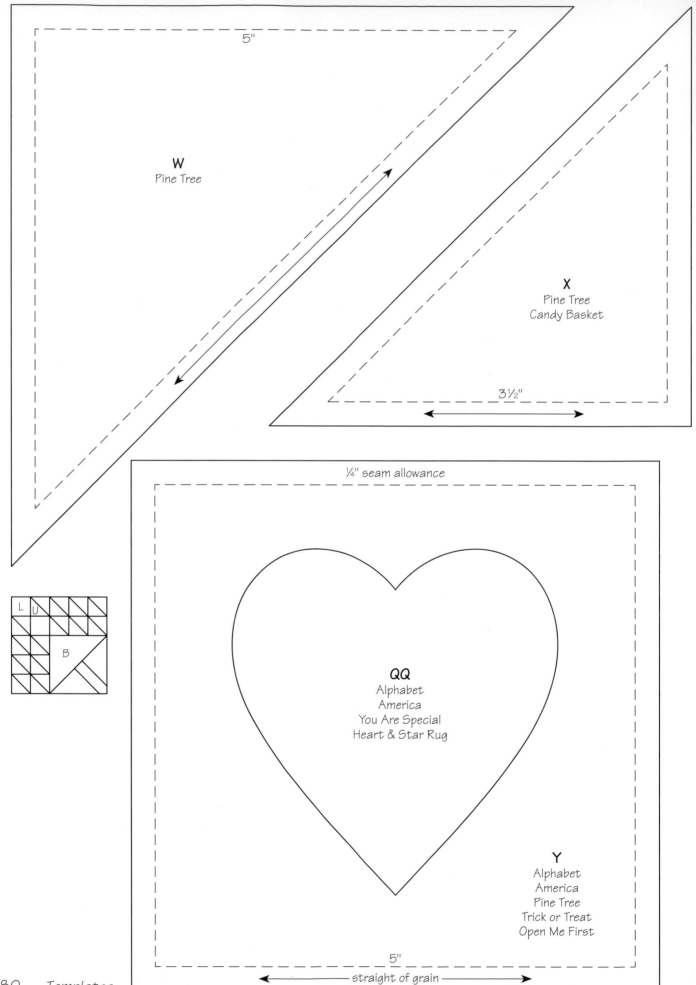

W
Pine Tree

5"

X
Pine Tree
Candy Basket

3½"

¼" seam allowance

L U

B

QQ
Alphabet
America
You Are Special
Heart & Star Rug

Y
Alphabet
America
Pine Tree
Trick or Treat
Open Me First

5"

straight of grain

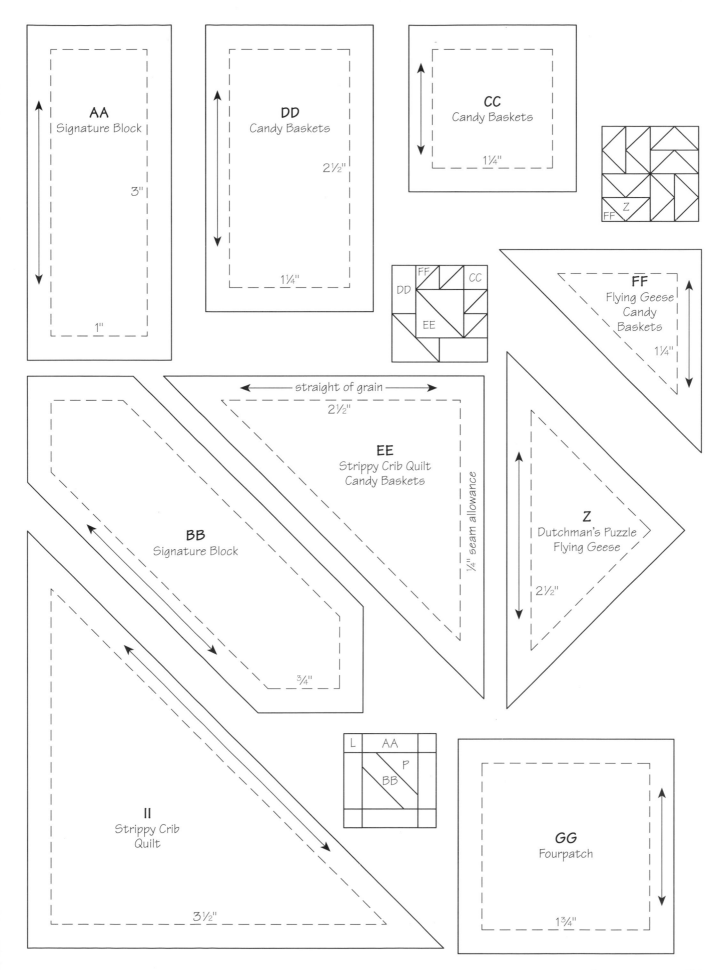

AA
Signature Block

3"

1"

DD
Candy Baskets

2½"

1¼"

CC
Candy Baskets

1¼"

Z

FF

FF | CC
DD | |
EE

FF
Flying Geese
Candy
Baskets

1¼"

straight of grain

2½"

EE
Strippy Crib Quilt
Candy Baskets

¼" seam allowance

BB
Signature Block

¾"

Z
Dutchman's Puzzle
Flying Geese

2½"

L | AA
| P
BB

II
Strippy Crib
Quilt

3½"

GG
Fourpatch

1¾"

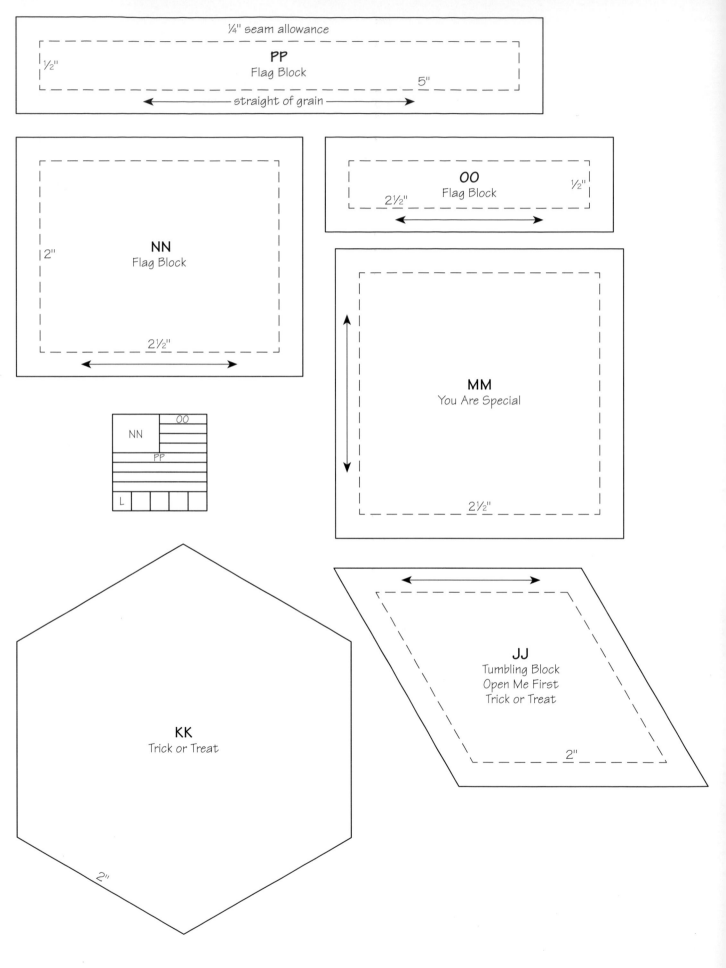

¼" seam allowance

PP
Flag Block

½"

5"

← straight of grain →

NN
Flag Block

2"

2½"

OO
Flag Block

2½"

½"

MM
You Are Special

2½"

| OO |
| NN |
| PP |
| L |

KK
Trick or Treat

2"

JJ
Tumbling Block
Open Me First
Trick or Treat

2"

Country House and Bird Rug

Hat

Snowman Rug and
Snowman Quilt Templates

For quilt, add ¼"-wide
seam allowances to
snowman, hat, and scarf.

Scarf

Use chain stitch
to embroider hands.

Snowman

A Little Quilt
in Celebration of:

_____

Made by _____
Date _____

Country House and Bird Rug

Permission granted to photocopy this page for your use.

O P Q
R S T U
V W X
Y Z

Top

To make the templates the proper size, enlarge these pages 140% on a photocopy machine; then photocopy the resulting copy at 140%.

Permission granted to photocopy this page for your use.

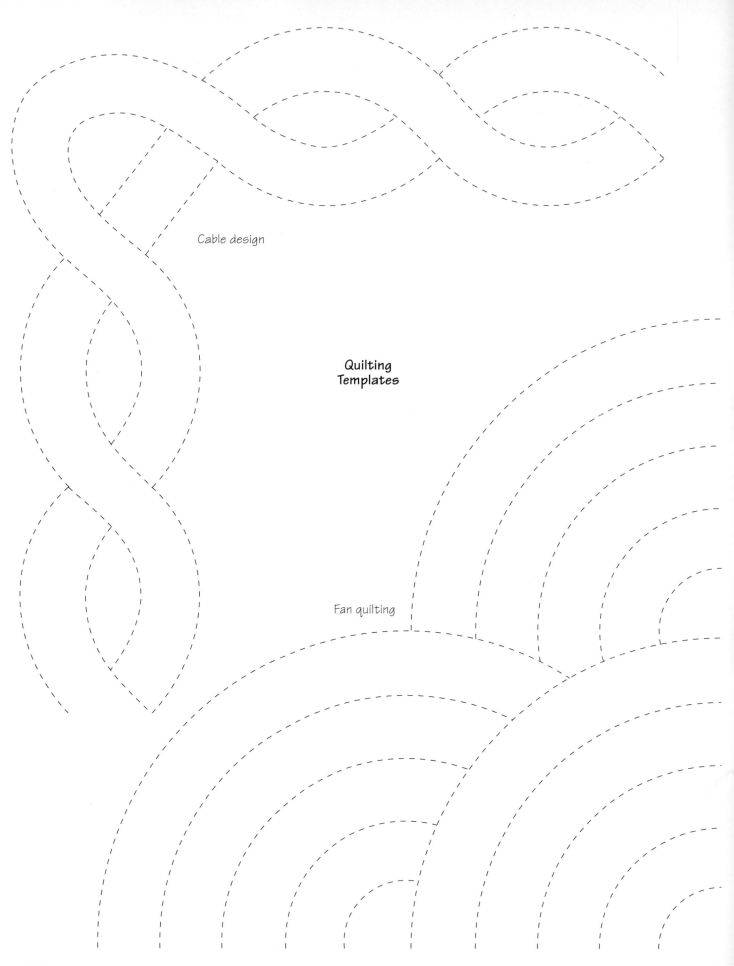

Cable design

Quilting
Templates

Fan quilting